LOLA'S

A CAKE JOURNEY AROUND THE WORLD

LOLA'S

A CAKE JOURNEY
AROUND THE WORLD

*70 of the most delicious and iconic cake recipes
discovered on our travels*

photography by
STEVE PAINTER

RYLAND PETERS & SMALL
LONDON • NEW YORK

For 'Omi' Vera Budwig devoted Mother, Grandmother and Great Grandmother, whose delicious recipes have always inspired us to cook and bake.

Mario and Asher – Lola's Cupcakes

Design, photography and prop styling Steve Painter
Editors Kate Eddison and Alice Sambrook
Head of Production Patricia Harrington
Art Director Leslie Harrington
Editorial Director Julia Charles
Publisher Cindy Richards

Recipe writer and developer Julia Head
Food Stylist Lucy McKelvie
Indexer Hilary Bird
US recipe tester and conversions Cathy Seward

First published in 2017
by Ryland Peters & Small
20–21 Jockey's Fields
London WC1R 4BW
and
341 East 116th Street
New York NY 10029

www.rylandpeters.com

Text © Lola's Cupcakes Ltd.
Design and commissioned photography © Ryland Peters & Small 2017. For other picture credits see page 191.

ISBN: 978-1-84975-809-3

10 9 8 7 6 5 4 3 2 1

Printed in Slovenia.

CIP data from the Library of Congress has been applied for. A CIP record for this book is available from the British Library.

Notes
• Both British (Metric) and American (Imperial plus US cup) measurements are included for your convenience, however, it is important to work with one set of measurements and not alternate between the two within a recipe.
• Eggs and butter should be used at room temperature.
• All spoon measurements are level, unless otherwise specified.
• Ovens should be preheated to the specified temperature. Recipes were tested using a fan oven. If using a conventional oven, follow the manufacturer's instructions for adjusting temperatures.
• All butter is unsalted, unless otherwise specified.
• All eggs are free-range and large (UK) or extra-large (US), unless otherwise specified. Recipes containing raw or partially cooked egg should not be served to the very young, very old, anyone with a compromised immune system or pregnant women.
• When using the zest of citrus fruit, try to find organic or unwaxed fruits and wash well before using.

Contents

Welcome to the world of LOLA'S baking

Lola's is a business with a simple aim: to handcraft the most delicious cakes you have ever tasted, using only the finest fresh ingredients. It is run with passion and creativity by Asher Budwig, a fourth-generation baker who grew up watching his father Mario establish the enormously successful chain Millie's Cookies. A knack for baking and entrepreneurial spirit clearly runs in the family, as Asher's grandmother and great grandmother also ran a pâtisserie and café in the 1940s in Colombia. With such a talented family of bakers, it is no wonder that Lola's continues to go from strength to strength.

Initially famous as the go-to place for stylish and delicious cupcakes, Lola's has expanded its range of baked goods. As well as fabulous cupcakes, they now offer a new and exciting range of large cakes to share and celebrate with, taking great inspiration from cakes around the world. A multi-national company, Lola's team of highly skilled bakers cover many countries, and all cultures add something different to the Lola's baking repertoire.

In this book, Lola's pass on their baking expertise with a deliciously diverse selection of recipes. From classic sponges to pastries, sweet breads, gateaux and traybakes, there is something for every baker, whether a simple cake to serve with mid-morning coffee or an extravagantly decorated party centrepiece. To help you on your baking journey, a helpful difficulty rating for these recipes indicates the level of skill involved: one whisk means the recipe is quick, easy and ideal for beginners, two whisks means the recipe has a few more steps to follow, and three whisks means the recipe will be quite advanced or time-consuming. However, nothing in the book is out of reach for the home-baker, even the cakes with three whisks are managable enough when the steps are followed with a little patience and care. There is also a selection of gluten-free and dairy-free cakes just to make sure that no one is left out! What are you waiting for – get your apron on and start your cake journey with Lola's.

Cakes of the world

Lola's bakery would like to take you on a deliciously sweet journey through Northern and Southern Europe, the Middle East, Africa, the Americas, the Caribbean, Australasia and Asia, all through the power of cake.

In these pages, you will find flavours and textures from afar that we hope will conjure up memories of trips past, or may even inspire you to travel further.

Food in itself is powerfully evocative, and can take you right back to a particular place and time as if it were yesterday. A vivid memory of a taste, texture or scent can all help to shape our adventures in life.

We can all remember an event as a child that ended in an unforgettable sweet treat. Perhaps it was the first French éclair from a real pâtisserie or a piece of rich chocolate cake at the local café.

Julia, our head recipe developer for this book, has such fond memories of holidays spent in France with daily runs to the patisserie to buy a tempting slice of *tarte aux pommes*. More recently, a hunt for the perfect mud cake inspired by an elusive version tasted in Australia – harder than you may think! What is clear is the significance of food, and often in particular cake, in our lives.

From East to West, everyday to avant-garde, cake of some kind has a place in most cultures. By sharing some of the most famous cakes from each country and snippets of the stories and legends behind them, we hope to express the heart-warming part that baking plays in bringing people together to share something homemade and full of tradition.

Although many of our recipes are loyal to classic methods and ingredients, we know how important traditional versions can be to a culture; therefore we are not trying to recreate 'Nona's' tiramisu word for word, instead we are here to open your senses to new and exciting flavours that the world has to offer. We like to give our own special Lola's touch to many of the recipes and bring some of them up to date where we see fit.

Cakes carry so much symbolism and meaning for a culture and can be inspired

by many things: significant ingredients, public holidays, celebrations or events in history. Important cakes have taken centre stage at social events for centuries. We have found that the key prized ingredients for each culture vary dramatically across the continents; for example, the Russian love for honey, the German love of Kirsch and the Greek fondness for lemon and olive oil have all inspired cakes in this book. What's more, there are huge variations in the textures, styles and decoration of cakes around the world.

This book covers them all, from the light cakes of Southern Europe such as the Genoise Sponge with Raspberries (see page 71), to the sometimes denser cakes of Northern Europe such as Parkin (see page 23) or Stollen (see page 48). Cakes from the Middle East often feature a richness that comes from being soaked in syrup with plenty of spices and dried fruits, in keeping with the wonderfully fragrant surrounds and methods of cooking in these countries. The cakes of Africa tend to heavily feature nuts and fruits, such as the Peanut and Banana Cake (see page 117). Across the Atlantic

we have wonderful creations from America, which tend to be sweet and often sponge-based. Undoubted world-renowned classics such as Red Velvet Cake (see page 123) and New York Cheesecake (see page 124) are iconic in their own right. Travelling further south to the Caribbean, they unsurprisingly take huge inspiration from the abundance of spices and tropical fruits. Strong flavours give these bakes wonderful warmth much like the tropical islands themselves. Next, we travel across to Australasia, where the bakes are more European in their history. Sponges laced with macadamia nuts or dark/bittersweet chocolate give slightly denser bakes in Australia and New Zealand. Finally, delicate yet exotic flavours such as matcha, sesame and mango, feature in the bakes of Asia.

Despite the vast variations in textures and flavours throughout this book, what remains the same all the way through is the pleasure that can be taken when eating that first bite. This feeling is universal the world over – pure happiness and escapism. What better way to travel the world than from your kitchen – and no jet lag!

Storecupboard essentials

Here is a list of some basic ingredients that feature throughout the book and how to use them. Baking is a science, and when combined correctly, these simple components can create wonderful things.

FLOUR
The variety most commonly used in our recipes is plain/all-purpose flour; it makes beautiful light sponges and is readily available. On occasion we instruct to use self-raising flours, which include a pre-mixed raising agent. For our American bakers, we sometimes suggest cake flour; this is a fine, light blend of flour commonly found in the US but not so readily available elsewhere; it has a low protein content so is great for making light sponges. Wholemeal/whole-wheat flour is used when we want a coarser texture and wholesome taste to cakes, it is usually combined with a little plain/all-purpose flour too. Occasionally, cornflour/cornstarch or polenta or fine cornmeal is used in place of or as well as flour, both of these are gluten-free and give a shorter more crumbly texture to your cake. For some cakes we have used white strong/bread flour, which contains a lot of gluten and gives a bouncy bread-like spring.

BUTTER
It is best to take butter out of the fridge at least 20 minutes before using to allow it to come to room temperature. We always use the unsalted variety, unless stated. This means you can be in control of the salt content of your baked goods. Sometimes we will instruct to add a little salt, where needed, as it can really lift the flavours.

EGGS
We use large UK or extra-large US free-range eggs in all our recipes. Again, we find that adding eggs at room temperature gives the best results.

SUGAR
Caster/granulated sugar is the most frequently used in baking for its neutral flavour. Light soft brown sugar gives a richer, more caramel-like flavour, but will add moisture and result in a heavier bake. Dark soft brown sugar has a strong treacly flavour – ideal in fruit cakes or gingerbread. Icing/confectioners' sugar is used mainly in frostings and finishing of cakes. We also sometimes use honey to sweeten in place of sugar.

RAISING AGENTS
Baking powder is a common addition to our bakes. A ready-made mix of cream of tartar and bicarbonate of soda/baking soda, it reacts with heat to produce carbon dioxide bubbles. If you don't have baking powder to hand, bicarbonate of soda/baking soda reacts with acidic ingredients such as lemon juice to similar effect.

VANILLA EXTRACT
Used in the majority of our bakes, this must be the extract variety and NOT the synthetic essence sometimes found in stores. Proper vanilla gives a mellow, sweet scent to your bakes.

Tools and basic equipment

When baking, it is important to read through the recipe before you start and make sure you have the right equipment to hand. The last thing you need is to get half way through a recipe and realize that you don't actually own a whisk! We have compiled a list of indispensable equipment for the home-baker.

RUBBER SPATULA
Useful for scraping down the bowl and incorporating ingredients into a batter.

SIEVE/STRAINER
Important to remove any lumps from dry ingredients and to remove seeds from fruit purées.

BALLOON WHISK
Useful when whipping cream or egg whites and for folding these into icings/frostings or batters.

A GOOD SET OF SCALES
We prefer to use electronic scales as they are accurate at measuring liquids and solids. Baking is a science so it is important that your ingredients are accurately measured.

A SET OF MEASURING SPOONS
Again, crucial in keeping measurements exact and for adding baking powders or spices.

A SELECTION OF MIXING BOWLS
One large and a few smaller heatproof bowls.

STAND MIXER
A stand mixer is every home cook's dream! We all covet the beautiful vintage mixers we see in the shops, however, there are cheaper models on the market that do just as good a job and are very reasonably priced. A stand mixer cuts baking preparation time in half; however, with a little elbow grease all our recipes can be made by hand. Most mixers will come with a paddle attachment, which is what we use when mixing our batters. Occasionally, we will use the whisk attachment, mainly when beating eggs with sugar.

HAND-HELD ELECTRIC MIXER
A hand-held electric mixer, the cousin of the stand mixer, is essential when whisking egg whites over heat, and it can be used instead of a stand mixer when preparing our batters. A very useful piece of kit, it is relatively inexpensive to buy.

A VARIED SELECTION OF CAKE PANS
We mainly use 23-cm/9-inch round loose-bottom or springform cake pans, as these produce a good-sized sponge and allow you to release the cakes easily and cleanly, which is particularly useful for delicate gateaux and layered cakes. Smaller 20-cm/8-inch round cake pans are useful for dainty teatime cakes such as a Victoria Sponge (see page 20). Other pans used in this book include loaf pans for making things like the Banana Bread (see page 120) and a square or rectangular brownie pan for traybake-style cakes such as Nanaimo Bars (see page 132). If you don't have exactly the correct pan size to hand, you can experiment with the pan sizes that you do have, but remember to adjust cooking times and temperatures accordingly.

BAKING PARCHMENT
This is an essential piece of kit in our kitchens. We like to use a silicone-lined, non-stick paper as this gives us certainty that our cakes will not stick while baking. You can also buy pre-cut circles and squares that neatly fit into the base of your pans in various sizes.

PALETTE KNIFE OR METAL SPATULA
We often instruct to use these for spreading frosting onto cakes neatly and evenly.

Specialist equipment and ingredients

Most equipment and ingredients in this book are readily available to the home-cook. There are a few things, however, we have not been able to locate within our local stores and may require you to shop online or use a specialist baking outlet.

BUNDT PANS AND MOULDS
Some recipes in this book feature cakes baked in special European-style Bundt pans. Most of these ornately-shaped cake pans are now readily available from good cookshops and even homeware departments. We have found that we get brilliant results from the silicone versions as they give a really clean edge to the shapes. However, the traditional-style metal pans also work well as long as they are greased properly (see below).

CAKE RELEASE SPRAY
When using intricate cake pans such as the Bundt pans, we have found that using a cake release spray really helps to remove the cooked cake quickly and easily. The spray really gets into the nooks and crannies of the pans, where standard buttering can sometimes fail.

PIPING NOZZLES/TIPS
You can buy piping nozzles/tips quite easily in stores. However, we like to source our piping nozzles/tips online because we find that the nozzles/tips supplied in home-baking kits can be too small. But please do experiment as you go, the style of finish is really up to you.

PIPING/PASTRY BAGS
We like to buy large disposable piping/pastry bags – a personal preference and a lot less mess when cleaning up! However, you can also buy a re-usable version, these tend to be made of strong material and are great for piping stiff icings. A third option is to construct a piping/pastry bag out of baking parchment – simply cut out a large triangle, roll into a cone shape and tape or staple to secure. You can also choose to forgo a piping/pastry bag altogether and just spoon or spread icing on instead. There are only a few cakes, such as the Millefeuille (see page 64) where the piping/pastry bag is really essential to the overall structure of a cake.

FOOD COLOURING
These can vary hugely from brand to brand. Most colourings for the domestic market are based on natural colourings, which, in our experience, do not give vibrant shades. We would advise to try online retailers for when brighter colours are needed. For example, the food colouring used in our Red Velvet Cake (see page 123) is sourced online as most domestic colours, in our experience, do not give a vibrant enough red shade to cut through the brown cocoa and chocolate in the sponge.

Baking tips

BATTERS AND MIXING

There are a few stages involved in preparing the perfect cake batter. We hope by providing you with a few tips, your baking experience will be simple and stress-free!

The most important thing to do before you start is make sure that all your ingredients are at room temperature – we can't stress how important this is! Take butter and eggs out of the fridge 20 minutes before you start. If you are short on time, you can bring cold eggs up to room temperature by placing them in a bowl filled with tepid water. Cold butter can be cut into small pieces and placed in a very low microwave or saucepan to soften. Do not leave raw eggs at room temperature for longer than 30 minutes, and use immediately once at room temperature.

The first stage with most of our recipes is to 'cream' the butter and sugar together. This really just means to beat the softened butter with the sugar and incorporate a little air. If you have time, this can be done by hand with a wooden spoon, but it is much quicker and easier to do it in a stand mixer with the paddle attachment or using a hand-held electric whisk and large mixing bowl.

Next, we add the eggs, one at a time, mixing slowly until incorporated. Do not worry if your mixture curdles after adding the eggs, this is very common and will normally be rectified once you have added the dry ingredients.

The dry ingredients are then added, but these must be sifted well first. At this stage, you can add any extras, such as nuts or chocolate.

We also use an 'all-in-one' method where all the ingredients are added at the same time and given a thorough mix to produce a smooth batter.

Finally, do not forget to preheat your oven at least 15 minutes before you plan to bake, and resist the urge to open the oven door until the baking time is complete. All these steps should help ensure your finished product is perfect.

ICINGS/FROSTINGS AND FINISHES

There are many different types of icing to try in this book. Every cake you create will look slightly different to the last one, but this is the best part about home-made cakes and hand-decorating them! We have used a mixture of buttercreams, cream cheese frostings, simple glazes and chocolate ganaches in our finishes. The toppings have been paired with the cakes to create the best flavour combinations possible. For example, the cool cream cheese frosting works well with the rich chocolate in the Stout Cake (see page 36) and a slightly sour Greek yogurt topping works well on the sweet Honey and Orange Cake (see page 87). Some cakes like the Brazil Nut Cake (see page 144) are simple everyday cakes that don't need a topping. Occasion cakes like the Banoffee Cake (see page 27) are finished with luxurious toppings (often piped) for a decadent finish.

Northern Europe

Victoria sponge ENGLAND

Parkin ENGLAND

Coffee and walnut cake ENGLAND

Banoffee cake ENGLAND

Marmalade cake SCOTLAND

Chocolate whisky cake SCOTLAND

Bara brith WALES

Stout cake IRELAND

Speculoos cake NETHERLANDS

Oliebollen NETHERLANDS

Dutch apple cake NETHERLANDS

Black forest cake GERMANY

Stollen GERMANY

Sacher torte AUSTRIA

Apple and sour cherry strudel AUSTRIA

Dobos torte HUNGARY

Babka POLAND

Marble cake DENMARK

Tarte tatin FRANCE

Paris-brest FRANCE

Millefeuille FRANCE

Victoria sponge ENGLAND

A real British classic. In our opinion you can't go wrong with a slice of Victoria sponge and a cup of tea as an afternoon treat. Here we have decorated our cake simply with a traditional dusting of icing/confectioners' sugar, however, you can choose to add fresh berries and cream for a more decorative finish. Whichever way you choose to adorn your cake, we are sure you will enjoy it!

CAKE

225 g/2 sticks butter, softened

225 g/1 cup plus 2 tablespoons caster/granulated sugar

1 teaspoon pure vanilla extract

4 eggs

225 g self-raising flour/1¾ cups cake flour mixed with 4 teaspoons baking powder, sifted

2 teaspoons baking powder

FILLING

140 g/1 cup fresh raspberries

2 tablespoons raspberry jam/jelly

80 g/½ cup fresh strawberries, stalks removed, finely chopped

200 ml/⅔ cup double/heavy cream, lightly whipped

TO DECORATE

1 teaspoon icing/confectioners' sugar, sifted

2 x 20-cm/8-inch sandwich cake pans, greased and lined with baking parchment

MAKES 1 MEDIUM CAKE

Preheat the oven to 180°C (350°F) Gas 4.

This cake uses an all-in-one method. Place all of the cake ingredients into the bowl of a stand mixer fitted with the paddle attachment (or use a hand-held electric whisk and large mixing bowl) and beat slowly to mix the ingredients together. Once mostly incorporated, stop the mixer and scrape down the sides of the bowl. Give the batter another good mix for 10–20 seconds to make sure all the flour has been incorporated and the mixture is smooth.

Divide the batter evenly between the prepared cake pans and bake in the preheated oven for 20–25 minutes or until well risen and a skewer inserted into the centre of the cake comes out clean. Turn out and allow to cool completely on a wire rack before decorating.

While the cakes are cooling, make the filling. Place the fresh raspberries into a bowl and, using a fork, mash them lightly to break them up slightly and allow the juices to run. Stir in the jam/jelly and finely chopped fresh strawberries, mixing until blended. Set aside. In another bowl whip the double/heavy cream to soft peaks.

Place one cooled sponge the right way up on a serving plate. Spoon the raspberry filling on top, spreading it almost to the edge. Turn the other sponge over and spread two-thirds of the cream onto the bottom (flat side) of this sponge, spreading it almost to the edge. Now take this sponge and carefully invert it cream-side down onto the raspberry layer – with a gentle press you should see the cream and jam/jelly filling at the edges of the cake. It does not matter if some of the filling oozes out.

Finish by dusting generously with icing/confectioners' sugar to decorate. You can of course decorate the sponge in any way that you choose. Take a large slice and enjoy!

Parkin ENGLAND

Parkin is traditionally made in the north of England for eating on cold frosty nights such as Bonfire night (November 5th). Spicy and laced with treacle/molasses, the flavours in the cake definitely improve with a few days storage tightly wrapped and hidden away. However, we like to eat it all year round and not just in the winter!

200 g/1½ cups plain/all-purpose flour

140 g/1 cup wholemeal/whole-wheat flour

1 teaspoon mixed spice/apple pie spice

1 teaspoon ground ginger

pinch of salt

1½ teaspoons bicarbonate of soda/baking soda

2 teaspoons freshly grated root ginger

170 g/2 cups rolled/jumbo oats

170 g/1 cup steel-cut pinhead oatmeal/oats

225 g/2 sticks butter

260 g/⅔ cup black treacle/molasses

170 g/¾ cup plus 1½ tablespoons soft dark brown sugar

220 ml/¾ cup full-fat/whole milk

2 eggs, lightly beaten

23-cm/9-inch square baking pan, greased and lined with baking parchment

MAKES 16 SMALL PIECES

Preheat the oven to 160°C (325°F) Gas 3.

Sift together the flours, spices, salt and bicarbonate of soda/baking soda into a large mixing bowl. Stir in the root ginger and both types of oats.

Place the butter, treacle/molasses and sugar into a pan and heat on medium heat until melted and the sugar has dissolved. Remove from the heat and allow to cool slightly.

Add the milk to the dry ingredients, followed by the eggs and the slightly cooled pan contents. Mix together briskly until smooth and pour into your prepared baking pan. Place in the centre of the preheated oven and bake for 50 minutes or until risen and a skewer inserted into the centre of the cake comes out clean.

Allow to cool in the pan for 20 minutes, then turn out onto a wire rack and remove the baking parchment. Once completely cool, cut into small squares and enjoy.

Coffee and walnut cake ENGLAND

A truly iconic British cake, present on many an afternoon tea display. Our coffee and walnut is fragrant with espresso and strewn with crunchy chopped walnuts. We think it is a delightful addition to a perfect afternoon tea.

CAKE

200 g/1¾ sticks butter, softened

200 g/1 cup soft light brown sugar

4 eggs

200 g self-raising flour/1½ cups cake flour mixed with 3 teaspoons baking powder

2 teaspoons baking powder

100 g/1 cup chopped walnuts

2 tablespoons instant espresso granules

BUTTERCREAM

150 g/1¼ sticks butter, softened

350 g/2½ cups icing/confectioners' sugar, sifted

1½ tablespoons milk

4 teaspoons instant espresso granules

TO DECORATE

chopped walnuts

2 x 23-cm/9-inch round loose-bottom or springform cake pans, greased and lined with baking parchment

MAKES 1 LARGE CAKE

Preheat the oven to 180°C (350°F) Gas 4.

Place all of the cake ingredients into the bowl of a stand mixer fitted with a paddle attachment (or use a hand-held electric whisk and large mixing bowl). This is known as an all-in-one method of making a cake batter. Beat together until well combined.

Divide the mixture evenly between the prepared cake pans and spread out with a spatula. Bake in the preheated oven for 45–55 minutes until a skewer inserted into the centre of the cakes comes out clean. Allow to cool in the pans for 5 minutes before turning out onto a wire rack to cool. Peel off the baking parchment.

For the buttercream, place the butter into the bowl of a stand mixer fitted with a paddle attachment (or use a hand-held electric whisk and mixing bowl) and beat until fluffy. Gradually add the icing/confectioners' sugar in stages with the mixer running on low speed. When all of the icing/confectioners' sugar is combined, add the milk and instant espresso granules and beat on medium speed until the buttercream is smooth.

When the cakes have cooled, spread half of the coffee buttercream on one cake and place the other cake on top. Spread the remaining buttercream on top of the cake and sprinkle the outside edge with chopped walnuts to decorate.

Banoffee cake ENGLAND

The banoffee pie was originally created at the Hungry Monk restaurant in East Sussex, England by owner Nigel Mackenzie and chef Ian Dowding. We have decided to recreate this delicious dessert into a showstopper of a cake.

230 g/2 sticks butter, melted

340 g/1¾ cups minus ½ tablespoon caster/granulated sugar

2 teaspoons pure vanilla extract

4 eggs

5 very ripe bananas (approximately 750 g/1 lb. 6 oz.), mashed with a fork

450 g/scant 3½ cups plain/all-purpose flour, sifted

2 teaspoons baking powder

1 teaspoon bicarbonate of soda/baking soda

BUTTERCREAM

350 g/3 sticks butter, softened

1 teaspoon pure vanilla extract

500 g/4¼ cups icing/confectioners' sugar, sifted

2 tablespoons milk

TO DECORATE

1 397-g/14-oz. can ready-made caramel

3 small bananas, sliced

3 x 23-cm/9-inch round loose-bottom or springform cake pans, greased and lined with baking parchment

2 large disposable piping/pastry bags

MAKES 1 LARGE CAKE

Preheat the oven to 180°C (350°F) Gas 4.

Start by creating the sponge layers. Place the melted butter, sugar and vanilla extract into the bowl of a stand mixer fitted with a paddle attachment (or use a wooden spoon and large mixing bowl) and beat on low speed to combine. Add the eggs, one at a time, stopping to scrape down the bowl occasionally. Carefully add the mashed bananas and combine. With the speed on low, slowly add the sifted flour, baking powder and bicarbonate of soda/baking soda, and mix on medium speed until just incorporated. Do not over-mix.

Divide the mixture evenly between the prepared cake pans and smooth the surface. Bake in the preheated oven for 20–25 minutes until well risen and a skewer inserted into the centre of each cake comes out clean. Remove from the oven, turn out onto a wire rack and leave to cool.

To make the buttercream, put the butter into the bowl of a stand mixer fitted with the paddle attachment (or use an electric hand-held whisk and a large mixing bowl) and beat until smooth. Add the vanilla extract and mix again. With the mixer on low speed, add half of the sifted icing/confectioners' sugar and slowly mix until all the sugar has been incorporated. Add the remaining sugar and beat again, still on low speed, until incorporated. You may find you have a cloud of sugar in your kitchen, but this is normal! Add the milk, a tablespoonful at a time, with the mixer on medium speed, beating until the icing is light and fluffy. Scrape the buttercream into the disposable piping/pastry bag using a spatula, and set aside.

Scrape the caramel into the second disposable piping/pastry bag. Place one of the sponge cakes onto a serving plate and carefully snip off 2.5 cm/1 inch from the bottom of the piping/pastry bag containing the buttercream. Pipe a ring of large splodges of buttercream around the edge of the sponge. Take the piping/pastry bag containing the caramel and do the same, piping inside the ring of buttercream.

Take half of the sliced bananas and place in the remaining circle of visible sponge to cover. Repeat with the next layer. Finish with the final layer of sponge and decorate using alternate rings of buttercream and caramel until the surface of the cake is covered.

Marmalade cake SCOTLAND

Marmalade and Scotland have a long history together. Created in the late 17th century, the delicious preserve has been gracing British breakfast tables for many years. This delicious marmalade cake is both bitter and sweet, and just gets better wrapped tightly and stored in an airtight container for a few days.

4 tablespoons soft light brown sugar

2 small oranges, peeled and sliced

6 tablespoons citrus marmalade

200 g/1¾ sticks butter

200 g/1 cup caster/granulated sugar

4 eggs

200 g self-raising flour/1½ cups cake flour mixed with 3 teaspoons baking powder

50 g/½ cup ground almonds

grated zest and juice of 1 orange

23-cm/9-inch round loose-bottom or springform cake pan, greased and lined with baking parchment

MAKES 1 LARGE CAKE

Preheat the oven to 160°C (325°F) Gas 3.

Start by sprinkling the brown sugar into the base of your prepared cake pan and arranging the fresh orange slices in a circular pattern on top of the sugar. This will be the top of your cake, so take some time to make it look beautiful.

Set aside 1 tablespoon of the marmalade for the glaze and place the remaining 5 tablespoons into the bowl of a stand mixer fitted with a paddle attachment (or use a hand-held electric whisk and large mixing bowl) along with all the other ingredients.

With the mixer running on low speed, combine the ingredients, turning the speed to medium for the final minute to make sure the batter is fully mixed.

Carefully spoon the batter on top of the orange slices in the cake pan and smooth over the top with your spatula. Bake in the preheated oven for 40–45 minutes until risen and springy to the touch.

Allow to cool in the pan for 15 minutes before carefully running a knife around the edge of the pan and inverting the cake onto a serving plate. This needs to be done when the cake is still warm to release all the yummy caramel orange juices on the base of the pan. Warm the reserved marmalade very briefly in the microwave until slightly loosened and then brush over the surface of the cake. Leave to cool completely before serving.

Chocolate whisky cake
SCOTLAND

300 g/2¼ cups plain/
all-purpose flour

400 g/2 cups caster/
granulated sugar

75 g/¾ cup unsweetened
cocoa powder

1½ teaspoons baking powder

1½ teaspoons bicarbonate of
soda/baking soda

½ teaspoon salt

2 eggs

230 ml/1 cup full-fat/whole
milk

115 ml/½ cup vegetable oil

1 teaspoon pure vanilla extract

230 ml/1 cup hot coffee

1 tablespoon Scotch whisky

WHISKY CREAM

1 tablespoon instant espresso
granules

3 tablespoons Scotch whisky

600 ml/3 cups double/heavy
cream

3 tablespoons soft light brown
sugar

TO DECORATE

dark/bittersweet chocolate
shavings

*3 x 23-cm/9-inch round loose-
bottom or springform cake
pans, greased and lined with
baking parchment*

MAKES 1 LARGE CAKE

The best combination ever. Combining the
smokiness of whisky with the rich dark
characteristics of chocolate cake is a match
made in heaven. We think our Scottish friends
will agree that this is a great way to showcase a
wonderful Scotch whisky. Delicious as a dessert
for a dinner party – or really at any time.

Preheat the oven to 180°C (350°F) Gas 4.

Place the flour, sugar, cocoa, baking powder, bicarbonate
of soda/baking soda and salt into the bowl of a stand mixer
fitted with a whisk attachment (or use a hand-held electric
whisk and large mixing bowl) and beat on low speed until well
blended together.

Add the eggs, milk, oil and vanilla extract and mix on low
speed, scraping down the sides of the bowl occasionally,
until the mixture is smooth. With the mixer running, gradually
add the hot coffee and whisky, mixing on low speed just until
combined. The batter will be quite thin.

Divide the batter equally between the prepared cake pans
and bake in the preheated oven for 25–30 minutes or until
well risen and a skewer inserted into the centre of each cake
comes out clean. Let the cakes cool completely in the pans
before turning out.

To make the whisky cream, put the espresso granules and
whisky in a bowl and stir together until completely dissolved.
Add to a large mixing bowl with the cream and brown sugar.
Whisk together for approximately 2 minutes until soft peaks
start to form.

Place one layer of sponge onto a serving plate and spread
one-third of the whipped cream on top, leaving a 1-cm/½-inch
border. Repeat with the second layer. Put the top sponge layer
in place and spread with the remaining whipped cream out to
the edge. Sprinkle the chocolate shavings around the outside
edge of the cake and serve.

Bara brith WALES

A nod to our dear Welsh friends. This delicious, fruity loaf cake retains its moisture and keeps in an airtight container brilliantly. Tea-soaked fruit adds depth of flavour and the addition of the Earl Grey tea gives a floral characteristic to the cake.

50 g/⅓ cup chopped dried pitted dates

150 g/1¼ cups sultanas/golden raisins

50 g/⅓ cup currants

100 g/¾ cup chopped dried apricots

210 g/1 cup soft light brown sugar

300 ml/1¼ cups hot, strongly brewed Earl Grey tea (or tea of your choice)

350 g self-raising flour/2⅔ cups cake flour mixed with 5 teaspoons baking powder

1 teaspoon mixed spice/apple pie spice

1 egg

2 tablespoons marmalade

900-g/2-lb. loaf pan, greased and lined with baking parchment

MAKES 1 LARGE LOAF CAKE

Measure the fruits and sugar into a bowl and pour over the hot tea. Cover and leave for at least 3 hours, or overnight if possible.

Preheat the oven to 150°C (300°F) Gas 2.

Sift the flour and spice into the fruit mixture, then stir in the egg followed by the marmalade. Mix until thoroughly combined and pour into the prepared cake pan. Level the surface with the back of a spoon.

Bake in the centre of the preheated oven for 1½–1¾ hours until a skewer inserted into the centre of the cake comes out clean. Allow to cool in the pan and then turn out. This can be served toasted with butter, but it is equally delicious just as it is.

Classic British Tea Rooms in
the Cotswolds, England (left).

Coffee with whipped cream and
a delicious apple strudel (above).

A café street sign
in Innsbruck,
Austria (right).

A Boulangerie-Patisserie in Provence-Alpes-Côte d'Azur, southern France (left).

Demel, a graceful, old-fashioned pastry shop in Vienna, Austria (below).

An ornate and beautiful coffee house in Budapest, Hungary (below).

Stout cake IRELAND

This cake has become a true favourite at Lola's. It really showcases the rich, dark nature of the classic Irish 'perfect pint'. By adding extra malt, we think we have created an even more sensational bake.

50 ml/3½ tablespoons dark Irish stout (we use Guinness)

250 g/2¼ sticks butter

400 g/2 cups white sugar

100 g/1 cup cocoa powder

30 g/3½ tablespoons malt powder (we use Horlicks)

150 ml/¾ cup sour cream

2 eggs

1 teaspoon pure vanilla extract

2 teaspoons bicarbonate of/ baking soda

275 g/2 cups plain/all-purpose flour

CREAM CHEESE FROSTING

25 g/¼ stick butter, softened

100 g/¾ cup icing/ confectioners' sugar

200 g/7 oz. cream cheese

grated chocolate, to decorate

23-cm/9-inch springform cake pan, greased and lined with baking parchment

MAKES 1 LARGE CAKE

Preheat the oven to 180°C (350°F) Gas 4.

Put the stout and butter in a large pan set over gentle heat. Don't let it boil, just let the butter melt through the liquid. Add the sugar, cocoa and malt powder to the warm butter-stout mixture and whisk gently to get rid of any lumps. Add the sour cream and stir in – this will cool the mixture sufficiently so that you can add the eggs and then the vanilla extract. Continue to mix until all the ingredients are completely incorporated.

Add the bicarbonate of soda/baking soda and then begin to add the flour, little by little, stirring each time until fully incorporated.

Pour the mixture into the prepared cake pan and bake in the preheated oven for 50–60 minutes. A skewer should come out clean when inserted into the centre. Turn out, them allow the cake to cool completely before decorating.

To make the cream cheese frosting, place the softened butter in a large bowl and add the icing/confectioners' sugar and cream cheese. Using a stand mixer or hand-held electric whisk, slowly and carefully beat everything together. Once combined, increase the speed and whip until you have a soft and fluffy frosting.

Place the cooled cake on your serving plate and loosely spoon over the frosting – we like to use a very informal swirl technique, but this is entirely up to you. Sprinkle around the top edge with grated chocolate to finish.

Speculoos cake NETHERLANDS

We first discovered the taste of speculoos while sitting in a café in Holland, in the form of the tiny delectable cookie served with our coffee. We then discovered that this treat had been made into a spread and knew that we had to utilize its flavour somehow. What resulted is this delicious layered creation. Thank you, Holland!

380 g/3 cups minus 2 tablespoons plain/all-purpose flour

2 teaspoons baking powder

pinch of salt

250 g/2¼ sticks butter, softened

400 g/2 cups caster/granulated sugar

grated zest of 1 orange

1½ teaspoons pure vanilla extract

4 eggs

180 ml/¾ cup full-fat/whole milk

60 ml/¼ cup freshly squeezed lemon juice

FROSTING

175 g/1½ sticks butter, softened

140 g/½ cup crunchy speculoos spread

140 g/½ cup smooth speculoos spread

300 g/2½ cups icing/confectioners' sugar, sifted

150 g/5 oz. full-fat cream cheese

CRUNCHY LAYER

200 g/⅔ cup crunchy speculoos spread

TOPPING

4 malted milk or caramel cookies, crumbled

2 x 23-cm/9-inch round loose-bottom or springform cake pans, greased and lined with baking parchment

MAKES 1 LARGE CAKE

Preheat the oven to 180°C (350°F) Gas 4.

In a large bowl, sift together the flour, baking powder and salt. Set aside. Place the butter, sugar, orange zest and vanilla extract into the bowl of a stand mixer fitted with the paddle attachment (or use a hand-held electric whisk and large mixing bowl) and beat together on medium speed until light and fluffy, about 2–3 minutes.

Add the eggs, one at a time, beating well after each addition. Add the flour mixture in three stages, alternating with the milk and lemon juice.

Spoon the batter into the prepared cake pans. Bake in the preheated oven for 35–40 minutes until a skewer inserted into the centre of the cakes comes out clean. Leave to cool in the pans for 15 minutes before turning out onto a wire rack to cool completely.

Using a serrated knife, slice horizontally through the middle of each sponge to create four even layers. Place the first layer on a serving plate ready to assemble.

For the frosting, place the butter into the bowl of a stand mixer fitted with the paddle attachment (or use a hand-held electric whisk and large mixing bowl) and beat on medium speed until light and fluffy, about 2–3 minutes. Add both the speculoos spreads and beat until well combined. Gradually beat in the sifted icing/confectioners' sugar. Slowly add the cream cheese, bit by bit, beating well after each addition.

Take one-third of the frosting and spread it on the first layer of sponge. Place another layer of sponge on top. Spread the additional crunchy layer of speculoos over the sponge. Place the next sponge layer on top and smooth over the next third of frosting. Place the final sponge layer on top of this and finish with the remaining frosting. If you have any speculoos spread left over in the jars, you can swirl this into the frosting for a lovely effect. Finish the top of the cake with crumbled cookies sprinkled along the outer edge. Enjoy!

Oliebollen NETHERLANDS

It seems that nearly every country you travel to has their own take on the classic doughnut. These wonderful fruity, light, almost rugged doughnuts are just delicious and we have the Dutch to thank for their creation. The addition of sharp apple and soft plump raisins makes these one of our favourite doughnuts of the world.

2¼ teaspoons active dried yeast

30 g/2½ tablespoons caster/granulated sugar

65 ml/¼ cup lukewarm water

225 g/1¾ cups plain/all-purpose flour

pinch of salt

125 ml/½ cup full-fat/whole milk

1 egg, lightly beaten

100 g/¾ cup (dark) raisins

1 small Granny Smith apple, peeled, cored and finely chopped

vegetable oil, for deep-frying

icing/confectioners' sugar, to decorate

deep fat fryer (optional)

MAKES 10 DOUGHNUTS

Place the yeast, sugar and lukewarm water into a small bowl and stir to dissolve. Set aside in a warm place for 10 minutes or until the mixture bubbles.

Place the flour and salt in a large bowl and make a well in the centre. Pour the milk, beaten egg and the yeast mixture into the well and stir until fully combined. Add the (dark) raisins and chopped apple and stir until well combined. The dough will be soft. Cover with clingfilm/plastic wrap and set aside in a warm, draught-free place for 1 hour or until the dough doubles in size. The dough will be quite soft and spoonable.

Fill a deep fat fryer or large, heavy-bottomed pan one-third full with vegetable oil and heat to 175°C (345°F) or until a cube of bread turns golden in 40 seconds. Working in batches, use two dessertspoons to scoop out a spoonful of the dough and gently drop it into the oil. Deep-fry, turning halfway, for 5 minutes or until golden and cooked through. Remove with a slotted spoon and drain on paper towels.

Dust the doughnuts generously with icing/confectioners' sugar and serve.

Dutch apple cake NETHERLANDS

Apple cake and Holland go hand in hand. There is evidence of an apple cake being found in a Dutch cookery book as far back as 1514. This delicious sponge allows the soft and sweet apples to rest on top as the crowning glory of this delicious treat.

100 g/7 tablespoons butter, softened

100 g/½ cup caster/granulated sugar

100 g/½ cup soft light brown sugar

1 egg

1 teaspoon pure vanilla extract

190 g/1½ cups minus 1 tablespoon plain/all-purpose flour

1½ teaspoons baking powder

½ teaspoon ground cinnamon

175 ml/¾ cup full-fat/whole milk

4 small dessert apples, peeled, cored and thinly sliced

30 g/⅓ cup flaked/slivered almonds

2 tablespoons good-quality apricot jam/jelly, sieved/strained

18-cm/7-inch square brownie pan, greased and lined with baking parchment

MAKES 1 CAKE

Preheat the oven to 160°C (325°F) Gas 3.

Place the butter and sugars into the bowl of a stand mixer fitted with a paddle attachment (or use a hand-held electric whisk and large mixing bowl) and beat on medium speed until light and fluffy. Beat in the egg and vanilla extract, stopping to scrape down the sides of the bowl occasionally. Sift the flour, baking powder and cinnamon into a separate bowl, and then add the dry ingredients to the batter, a spoonful at a time, alternating with the milk, until full incorporated and smooth. Do not over-mix.

Spread the cake mixture evenly into the prepared brownie pan and very carefully arrange the apple slices in lines over the top of the cake. We like to use one apple per line as this fits snugly in the pan. Take the flaked/slivered almonds and frame the apples around the edge of the pan.

Bake in the preheated oven for 50–60 minutes or until well risen and a skewer inserted into the centre of the cake comes out clean. Allow the cake to cool in the pan for 5 minutes before brushing the apricot jam/jelly over the surface to give a wonderful shiny finish. Remove from the pan and serve warm or at room temperature.

Black forest cake GERMANY

Also known as Schwarzwälder Kirschtorte, this delicious cake contains the ingredient it is so aptly named after, kirsch. The morello cherry liqueur adds a real depth of flavour. Turn to pages 46–47 to read more about this wonderful cake.

400 g/2 cups caster/granulated sugar

230 g/1¾ cups plain/all-purpose flour

120 g/1¼ cups unsweetened cocoa powder

1 teaspoon baking powder

2 teaspoons bicarbonate of soda/baking soda

180 ml/⅔ cup sour cream

4 eggs

2 tablespoons full-fat/whole milk

250 ml/1 cup cold strong coffee

100 ml/scant ½ cup vegetable oil

FOR THE CHERRY FILLING

grated zest from 1 large unwaxed orange

2 425-g/15-oz. cans black cherries in natural juice

50 g/¼ cup caster/granulated sugar

large pinch of ground cinnamon

2 tablespoons cornflour/cornstarch

FOR THE KIRSCH SYRUP

80 g/scant ½ cup caster/granulated sugar

5 tablespoons kirsch

FOR THE CREAM

1 teaspoon pure vanilla extract or paste

800 ml/scant 3½ cups double/heavy cream, softly whipped

TO DECORATE

dark/bittersweet chocolate curls

fresh cherries

icing/confectioners' sugar

23-cm/9-inch square or round loose-bottom or springform cake pan, greased and lined with baking parchment

piping/pastry bag fitted with a plain or star nozzle/tip (optional)

MAKES 1 LARGE CAKE

Preheat the oven to 160°C (325°F) Gas 3.

Sift the dry ingredients into a large bowl. Mix the sour cream, eggs, milk and coffee together in a separate bowl and slowly add the sifted dry ingredients. Whisk until the batter is smooth, then slowly beat in the vegetable oil.

Pour the batter into the prepared pan and bake in the preheated oven for 60–70 minutes until well risen and a skewer inserted into the centre of the cake comes out clean. Allow to cool in the pan for 10 minutes before turning out onto a cooling rack.

Meanwhile, make the cherry filling. Place the orange zest into a medium pan. Drain the juice from the cans of cherries and add to the saucepan. Add the sugar and cinnamon and bring to the boil, simmering for 5 minutes until reduced slightly. Mix the cornflour/cornstarch with a little water and whisk into the simmering juice. Simmer for 5 minutes until thickened and glossy. Remove the orange zest and add the canned cherries to

the syrup. Allow to cool fully before using.

To make the kirsch syrup, dissolve the sugar in 130 ml/½ cup water in a small pan over medium heat. Bring to the boil and simmer for 2 minutes. Remove from the heat, stir in the kirsch and then set aside to cool.

For the cream, gently fold the vanilla extract through the softly whipped cream and set aside.

To assemble, use a serrated knife to carefully cut the cooled cake horizontally into four layers.

Take the first layer of cake and brush liberally with the kirsch syrup. Spread a thin layer of cream over the sponge and place one-third of the cooled cherry mixture over the cream. Place the next layer of sponge on top of this and repeat with the remaining layers, gently pressing down as you go. Brush the final layer of cake with the remaining kirsch syrup and then pipe or spread a final layer of cream on top. Dot with fresh cherries and scatter with chocolate curls to finish.

Black Forest Gateau: the retro classic

Popularized outside of Germany in the 1970s, the delectable Black Forest Gateau (or sometimes cake) is still today one of the world's most popular desserts. Opinions differ over the reason for its name, the origin of the recipe, and its various incarnations, but it is usually comprised of several layers of chocolate sponge, moistened with kirsch and layered with cream or buttercream and morello cherries.

The German name Schwarzwälder Kirschtorte translates to 'Black Forest cherry torte' – a reference to the kirsch syrup that the sponge is doused in, which is produced in the Black Forest area of South West Germany. Further theories surrounding the reason for the name 'Black Forest' include the comparison of the dark chocolate sponge to the dark, thickly growing trees in the Black Forest. Another possible theory is the striking traditional costume worn by women in parts of the Black Forest: a black dress for the chocolate sponge, a white blouse for the cream and a hat featuring large cherry-red pom-poms (pictured right, above).

An integral part of the famous dessert, kirsch or kirschwasser is produced in areas of France and Switzerland as well as Germany, this leads some to think that older versions of the recipe may not necessarily be confined to Germany.

Some believe that the Schwarzwälder Kirschtorte was invented in Switzerland by Erwin Hildenbrand of the Café Walz in Tübingen in 1930. A conflicting and perhaps more well-known story is that it was invented around 1915 by confectioner Josef Keller, at Café Ahrend in Bad Godesberg in Bonn, Germany. No matter the precise origin, within a few years the Schwarzwälder kirschtorte was a staple at every German Konditorei, and within a few decades, people around the world fell in love with the cake, too. The flavour combination of cherries, kirsch, chocolate and cream remains a match made in heaven. Turn to page 44 to make our version of this world-famous cake.

Stollen GERMANY

Our stollen wreath is not only beautiful to look at but is deliciously moist and scrumptious to eat. Rich, spiced fruited dough conceals a wonderful marzipan/almond paste surprise and is bound to please over the festive season.

130 g/1 cup sultanas/golden raisins

130 g/1 cup (dark) raisins

1 teaspoon ground mixed spice/apple pie spice

½ teaspoon ground cinnamon

grated zest of 1 lemon

grated zest of 1 orange

4 teaspoons Calvados brandy (apple brandy)

250 ml/1 cup warm milk

12 g/½ oz. active dried yeast

500 g/3½ cups white strong/bread flour, sifted, plus extra for dusting

140 g/1¼ sticks unsalted butter

55 g/generous⅓ cup icing/confectioners' sugar, sifted, plus extra to decorate

1 egg

1 teaspoon salt

200 g/7 oz. store-bought marzipan/almond paste

ICING

100 g/½ cup icing/confectioners' sugar, sifted

dried fruit of your choosing (such as cranberries or raisins), to decorate (optional)

large baking sheet, lined with baking parchment

15-cm/6-inch round cake pan (or an ovenproof bowl covered in foil)

MAKES 1 LARGE WREATH

Place the sultanas/golden raisins, (dark) raisins, mixed spice/apple pie spice, cinnamon, lemon zest and orange zest in a bowl, cover with the brandy and leave to soak for 3 hours or overnight until the liquid has been all soaked up.

Mix the warm milk and yeast together and set aside for 10 minutes until frothy and bubbly.

In a separate bowl, rub the flour and butter together until the mixture resembles very fine breadcrumbs.

Add the icing/confectioners' sugar, egg and salt and then add the yeast mixture. Mix by hand (or using the paddle attachment of a stand mixer) to a smooth dough. Knead on a work surface for 10 minutes by hand (or 5 minutes in a mixer) until the dough is stretchy.

Carefully mix in the soaked fruit until evenly dispersed throughout the dough. Place the dough in a bowl with a damp kitchen cloth on top and leave to rise in a warm place for 30 minutes.

Remove the dough from the bowl and carefully stretch it into a long roll. With a sharp knife, cut two long slits, side by side, lengthways almost through the dough (do not handle the dough too much). Roll the marzipan/almond paste into two thin rolls and carefully place them into the slits, then pinch the two sides together to seal the slits shut, encasing the marzipan/almond paste. Roll the dough up into a fat sausage and shape into a ring. Press the ends together to seal.

Place on the prepared baking sheet and position the small round pan or foil-covered bowl in the middle, so the dough will remain in shape when baking. Leave to rise in a warm place with a damp kitchen cloth on top until it has doubled in size, about an hour.

Preheat the oven to 200°C (400°F) Gas 6.

Bake in the preheated oven for 20–25 minutes, then tap the bottom of the loaf – if it has a hollow sound it is cooked. Remove from the oven and allow to cool completely on the baking sheet.

To make the icing, stir 2–3 teaspoons cold water into the icing/confectioners' sugar and then drizzle lines over the cooled stollen, letting them drip down the sides of the wreath. Scatter with extra dried fruit of your choice to finish.

Sacher torte AUSTRIA

A true classic, this well-known chocolate cake is said to have been invented in Vienna by chef Franz Sacher in 1832. At Lola's we have added our own touch to the traditional recipe by incorporating a delicious mousse layer.

140 g/5 oz. dark/bittersweet chocolate (no more than 70% cocoa solids), chopped

140 g/1¼ sticks butter, softened

115 g/½ cup plus 1 tablespoon caster/granulated sugar

1 teaspoon pure vanilla extract

5 eggs, separated

85 g/¾ cup ground almonds

55 g/scant ½ cup plain/all-purpose flour, sifted

MOUSSE

150 g/3½ cups mini marshmallows

50 g/3½ tablespoons butter

250 g/9 oz. dark/bittersweet chocolate (no more than 70% cocoa solids), chopped

60 ml/¼ cup hot water

300 ml/1½ cups double/heavy cream

1 teaspoon pure vanilla extract

GANACHE

200 ml/⅔ cup double/heavy cream

140 g/5 oz. dark/bittersweet chocolate, chopped

TO ASSEMBLE

5 tablespoons apricot jam/jelly, strained

25 g/1 oz. milk chocolate

23-cm/9-inch round loose-bottom or springform cake pan, greased and lined with baking parchment

piping/pastry bag fitted with a small plain nozzle/tip

MAKES 1 LARGE CAKE

Preheat the oven to 180°C (350°F) Gas 4.

Place the chocolate in a heatproof bowl set over a pan of gently simmering water. Allow to melt, stirring occasionally. Leave to cool slightly.

Beat the butter until soft with a wooden spoon or a hand-held electric whisk. Slowly beat in the sugar until the mixture is light and fluffy. Beat in the cooled chocolate and vanilla extract followed by the egg yolks. Finally, fold in the ground almonds and sifted flour. The mixture will be quite thick.

In a separate bowl, whisk the egg whites until stiff. Add one-third to the chocolate mixture and stir in vigorously using a metal spoon. Gently fold in the remaining egg whites.

Pour the mixture into the prepared cake pan and smooth the surface. Bake in the preheated oven for 45–50 minutes or until well risen and springy. Allow to cool in the pan for a few minutes, then turn out onto a wire rack to cool completely.

To make the mousse, place the marshmallows, butter, chocolate and water into a heavy-bottomed pan and gently heat to melt the contents, stirring a little. Remove from the heat and allow to cool.

In another bowl, gently whip the double/heavy cream and vanilla extract until thick. Fold into the cooling mousse until smooth and silky. Set aside.

For the ganache, place the double/heavy cream into a pan and heat until almost bubbling. Pour the hot cream over the chopped chocolate and stir until smooth. Set aside to cool slightly.

Use a serrated knife to slice the sponge horizontally into three even layers. Place the first layer of cake onto the cooling rack (with a tray underneath to catch drips) and smooth over half of the apricot jam/jelly. Carefully add half of the mousse on top using a palette knife or metal spatula to spread to the edges. Repeat with the next layer of sponge, using all the jam/jelly and mousse before adding the top layer of sponge.

Pour the chocolate ganache over the cake and allow it to drizzle down the sides. Run a palette knife or metal spatula carefully over the top of the cake to push any excess ganache down and smooth around the sides. Allow to set at room temperature, before refrigerating for an hour or so.

Melt the milk chocolate in a heatproof bowl set over a pan of gently simmering water. Allow to cool slightly before carefully using it to pipe the word 'Sacher' on top of the finished cake.

Apple and sour cherry strudel AUSTRIA

For us, this Austrian classic is best enjoyed warm after a cold crisp morning walk, with a steaming cup of tea or coffee. Here at Lola's, we have tweaked the recipe to give a slightly more 'showy' finish, not that there is anything wrong with this delicious classic, of course! Feel free to add your favourite dried fruits or nuts or even spices to create your own bespoke flavour.

680g/1½ lb. dessert apples, peeled, cored and chopped (approximately 6 apples)

grated zest of ½ orange

1 tablespoon freshly squeezed orange juice

100 g/½ cup caster/granulated sugar

1½ tablespoons kirsch

pinch of ground nutmeg

½ teaspoon ground cinnamon

30 g/¼ cup sultanas/golden raisins

50 g/⅓ cup dried sour/tart cherries

6–8 sheets ready-made filo/phyllo pastry

55 g/½ stick butter, melted and cooled

2 tablespoons polenta or fine cornmeal

25 g/¼ cup flaked/slivered almonds

icing/confectioners' sugar, for dusting

large baking sheet, lined with baking parchment

MAKES 1 STRUDEL

Preheat the oven to 190°C (375°F) Gas 5.

Make the strudel filling by mixing together the apples, orange zest and juice, sugar, kirsch, nutmeg, cinnamon, sultanas/golden raisins and cherries. Set aside.

For the pastry, lightly brush one sheet of filo/phyllo with melted butter. Place onto the baking parchment on the baking sheet, butter-side up. Repeat with the remaining sheets, brushing each layer with butter as you go. Sprinkle the polenta or fine cornmeal over the buttered pastry, ready to place the apples on top. Carefully spoon the apple filling along the middle of the pastry layers, leaving 2.5 cm/1 inch at each end for folding.

Using the paper to assist you, roll the strudel into a large sausage shape, making sure the seal is tucked underneath. Carefully fold the ends underneath, brush with the remaining melted butter and sprinkle a neat line of flaked/slivered almonds along the top. Bake in the preheated oven for 40–45 minutes until the pastry is crisp and golden.

Dust with icing/confectioners' sugar and serve warm or cold.

Dobos torte HUNGARY

There are hundreds of variations of this famous classic, perhaps because the true recipe was not shared until 1906 when confectioner Jozsef Dobos retired and passed on his secrets. Our version is a real showstopper and worth the effort.

6 eggs, separated

1 teaspoon pure vanilla extract

150 g/1 cup icing/confectioners' sugar, sifted

30 g/⅓ cup unsweetened cocoa powder, sifted

100 g/¾ cup plain/all-purpose flour, sifted

grated zest of 1 orange

FROSTING

120 g/4 oz. dark/bittersweet chocolate (70% cocoa solids), chopped

5 egg yolks

150 g/¾ cup caster/granulated sugar

200 g/1¾ sticks butter, cut into small cubes

75 g/½ cup chopped hazelnuts

TO DECORATE

100 g/½ cup caster/granulated sugar

40 x 28-cm/16 x 11-inch baking tray, greased and lined with baking parchment

MAKES 1 LARGE TORTE

Preheat the oven to 180°C (350°F) Gas 4.

Place the egg yolks, vanilla extract and half the icing/confectioners' sugar into the bowl of a stand mixer fitted with a whisk attachment (or use a hand-held electric whisk and large mixing bowl). Beat on medium-high speed until fluffy and pale.

Place the egg whites and the remaining icing/confectioners' sugar into another mixing bowl and beat with an electric hand-held whisk on high speed until glossy and stiff peaks form.

Using a metal spoon, gently fold the egg whites into the yolk mixture, followed by the cocoa powder and half of the flour. Add the remaining flour and orange zest and mix carefully, trying not to knock out the air. Gently pour the batter into the prepared baking tray and spread level. Bake in the preheated oven for 12–15 minutes until risen and dry but still pale in colour. Quickly transfer the cake to a wire rack to cool and peel off the paper (otherwise it will carry on cooking in the hot tray).

For the frosting, melt the chocolate in a heatproof bowl set over a pan of barely simmering water. Place the egg yolks into the bowl of a stand mixer fitted with a whisk attachment (or use a hand-held electric whisk and large mixing bowl) and start to whisk on low speed.

Meanwhile, place the sugar into a small pan with 3 tablespoons water and heat until dissolved. Boil for 4 minutes without stirring. You do not want the syrup to brown like a caramel, just to thicken slightly. Very carefully pour the hot syrup over the egg yolks, beating on medium speed. Increase the speed and mix until the yolks are pale, fluffy and doubled in size. Lower the speed to medium and add the butter, one cube at a time. Fold in the melted chocolate until smooth and shiny.

Cut the cooled sponge into six equal strips. Place the first piece onto a serving plate. Spread with a little frosting and top with another layer of sponge. Repeat for the other five layers. Cover the top and sides of the cake with the remaining frosting using a warm palette knife or metal spatula. Press the hazelnuts into the top and sides of the cake. Refrigerate for an hour to firm up.

To decorate, dissolve the sugar with 2 tablespoons water in a saucepan over medium heat. Boil without stirring until it turns golden. Very carefully, use a teaspoon to drizzle swirls and patterns onto a sheet of greaseproof paper.

The caramel will set quickly and become brittle. When ready to serve, remove the cake from the fridge and decorate the top with caramel shapes.

Babka POLAND

This wonderful enriched yeasted cake is a real classic. You will need to start the bake early in the morning to allow all day for the dough to rise. Alternatively, the first prove can be done overnight in the fridge for a minimum of 12 hours.

100 ml/⅓ cup plus
1 tablespoon warm milk

180 g/1 cup minus 1½
tablespoons caster/granulated
sugar

3 teaspoons active dried yeast

500 g/3¾ cups plain/all
purpose flour, plus a little
additional for dusting

2 eggs

1 egg yolk

1 teaspoon vanilla extract

½ teaspoon salt

150 g/1¼ sticks butter, cut
into pieces and softened

EGG WASH

1 egg yolk

1 tablespoon milk

CHOCOLATE FILLING

80 g/¾ stick butter, softened

30 g/½ cup cocoa powder

100 g/3½ oz. dark/
bittersweet chocolate (no more
than 60% cocoa solids), finely
chopped

80 g/½ cup caster/granulated
sugar

1 teaspoon ground cinnamon

TO FINISH

30 g/⅛ cup runny honey

*900-g/2-lb. loaf pan, greased
and lined with baking
parchment*

MAKES ONE LARGE LOAF

Put the warm milk and 2 tablespoons of the sugar into the bowl of a stand mixer fitted with the paddle attachment. Sprinkle over the dried yeast and leave until bubbly, about 10 minutes. Add one-third of the flour to the yeast and beat at medium speed until combined. Add the eggs, yolk, vanilla, salt, and remaining sugar and beat until combined. Reduce the speed to low, and then mix in the remaining flour slowly. Increase the speed to medium, then beat in the softened butter, a little at a time. Beat until the dough is smooth and elastic, about 4 minutes.

Put the dough into a lightly oiled bowl and cover with clingfilm/plastic wrap. Leave in a warm place to rise until doubled in size, this can take up to 6 hours depending on the yeast, 4–5 hours is average.

Lightly oil your hands and push the air out of the risen dough. Roll out the dough on a floured work surface with a lightly floured rolling pin into a large rectangle, measuring roughly 50 x 30 cm/20 x 12 inches. Arrange with the long side nearest you. In a small bowl beat together the egg yolk and milk for the egg wash. Spread the softened butter onto your dough, leaving a border all around. Brush some of the egg wash onto the long border nearest you. Sift the cocoa onto the buttered dough, followed by the chopped chocolate and finally the sugar and cinnamon. Starting with the long side farthest from you, roll the dough into a snug log, pinching firmly along the egg-washed seam to seal. With a sharp knife cut a long slit through the dough 2.5 cm/1 inch from the end, all along the roll (quite deeply but not all the way through) to reveal the chocolate filling. Twist one end of the dough over the other several times to create a twisted rope. This is a bit fiddly but doesn't need to be perfect. Fold the rope back on itself so the dough is half the length and place in the prepared pan. Cover with clingfilm/plastic wrap and leave to rise again for 2–3 hours until the dough reaches the top of the pan.

Preheat the oven to 170°C (325°F) Gas 3.

Brush the risen dough with the remaining egg wash and bake in the centre of the preheated oven for 45–50 minutes. If the top of your loaf is darkening too quickly, cover it with foil in the final stages of baking. The loaf is cooked, once well risen and a skewer inserted comes out without any sticky raw dough, there may be a little chocolate, which is fine. Brush the loaf with the honey and be sure to cool to room temperature in the pan before removing and serving in thick slices.

Marble cake DENMARK

The marble cake was probably invented in Germany, however, it has become a real favourite Danish treat. By putting ground almonds in the batter, we have added extra moisture, creating a dark and light swirl of delicious sponge.

Preheat the oven to 160°C (325°F) Gas 3.

Start by sifting the flour and baking powder together in a mixing bowl. Place the butter, sugar, ground almonds, eggs, sour cream and vanilla extract into the bowl of a stand mixer fitted with the paddle attachment (or use a hand-held electric whisk and large mixing bowl) and mix to combine. Slowly add the sifted flour and baking powder and beat on high speed until fully incorporated.

In a small bowl, mix the cocoa powder and warm water together and set aside. Divide the cake batter in half, placing one half into a clean bowl. Add the cocoa mixture to this portion of batter to create your chocolate sponge, mixing well.

To create the marble effect, add spoonfuls of vanilla and chocolate batter alternately to the prepared cake pan. Run a kitchen knife through the batters to blend them gently into one another.

Bake in the preheated oven for 50–60 minutes or until a skewer inserted into the centre of the cake comes out clean. Allow the cake to cool in the pan for 30 minutes before turning out.

To make the glaze, place the double/heavy cream into a small saucepan and heat until just bubbling around the edges; we call this scalding point. Place the chocolate in a heatproof bowl and pour the hot cream over the top. Stir to melt the chocolate into the cream. Once the mixture is smooth, gently pour this over the surface of the cooled cake, allowing it to drip between the cracks and surface of the moulded shape. Allow to set for at least 1 hour before slicing and enjoying with a cup of tea!

300 g self-raising flour/2¼ cups cake flour mixed with 4 teaspoons baking powder

2 teaspoons baking powder

335 g/3 sticks butter, softened

335 g/1¾ cups minus 1 tablespoon caster/granulated sugar

115 g/1 generous cup ground almonds

6 eggs

3 tablespoons sour cream

1 teaspoon pure vanilla extract

2 tablespoons unsweetened cocoa powder, sifted

3 tablespoons warm water

GLAZE

300 ml/1¼ cups double/heavy cream

250 g/9 oz. dark/bittersweet chocolate (no more than 60% cocoa solids), chopped

26-cm/10½-inch *Kugelhopf, Bundt or decorative ring mould pan, greased and floured*

MAKES 1 LARGE CAKE

Tarte tatin FRANCE

The team at Lola's adore this iconic French dessert, which was created by sisters Stéphanie and Caroline Tatin at the Hotel Tatin in the 1880s. Softly caramelized apples nestle beneath a light puff pastry lid, until the brave moment of turning out the tarte to reveal the caramel goodness. With the addition of fresh thyme, this dessert is a real show-stopper.

250 g/9 oz. all-butter puff pastry

6 Granny Smith or Cox's apples

25 g/¼ stick butter

75 g/⅓ cup plus 2 teaspoons caster/granulated sugar

3 sprigs of fresh lemon thyme

plain/all-purpose flour, for dusting

23-cm/9-inch ovenproof frying pan/skillet

MAKES 1 TARTE

Preheat the oven to 200°C (400°F) Gas 6.

On a lightly floured surface, roll the pastry into a 30-cm/12-inch circle. Trim the circle to create a neat edge.

Peel, core and quarter the apples and set aside ready for use. Melt the butter in the ovenproof frying pan/skillet and add the caster/granulated sugar. Allow the sugar to dissolve without stirring, just swirl the butter and sugar together in the pan. Turn up the heat and allow the sugar to bubble and caramelize to a light brown colour. Remove from the heat at this stage, as the sugar will continue to turn darker as it cools slightly.

Carefully arrange the apples on top of the caramel in a tight spiral pattern, with the cut core side facing down. Strip the leaves from the thyme sprigs and scatter among the apples.

Place the puff pastry circle on top of the apples. Gently use a kitchen knife to nudge the pastry down and nestle it in and under the apples at the edge (this will create a lip once the tarte is turned out). Make a small slit in the top of the tarte to allow the steam to escape and place in the preheated oven for 30–35 minutes until the pastry is golden brown and puffed up.

Allow to cool in the frying pan/skillet for 5 minutes before carefully placing a serving plate that is slightly larger than your pan over the top and then swiftly turning it over to release the tarte onto the plate. Drizzle any juices or caramel over the apples and serve.

Paris brest FRANCE 🥄🥄🥄

The legendary Paris Brest is a strong, iconic symbol of two great French passions – patisserie and cycling. Here we have used an almond butter to flavour the rich, whipped filling, but you could also use a praline paste or chocolate hazelnut spread.

100 g/7 tablespoons butter

200 g/1½ cups plain/all-purpose flour

4 eggs, beaten

1 egg yolk, for brushing

50 g/½ cup flaked/slivered almonds

icing/confectioners' sugar, to decorate

FILLING

250 g/1¼ cups caster/granulated sugar

8 egg yolks

pinch of salt

250 g/2¼ sticks butter, softened and cut into small cubes

200 g/⅔ cup smooth almond butter

large baking sheet, lined with baking parchment

2 large piping/pastry bags, fitted with round nozzles/tips

sugar thermometer

MAKES 1 LARGE TART

Preheat the oven to 180°C (350°F) Gas 4.

Place the butter and 250 ml/1 cup plus 1 tablespoon water into a saucepan and heat until bubbling. Remove from the heat and add all the flour in one go. Using a wooden spoon, beat rapidly to bring the choux paste together until smooth. Return to gentle heat and cook for a few minutes to remove the taste of raw flour.

Transfer the choux paste into the bowl of a stand mixer fitted with the paddle attachment (or use a hand-held electric whisk and large mixing bowl) and allow to cool for 10 minutes. Beat the paste until soft, smooth and almost cool. Carefully drizzle in the beaten eggs and beat until smooth and elastic.

Scrape the choux paste into a piping/pastry bag. Carefully pipe a large circle (about 23 cm/ 9 inches) onto the parchment-lined baking sheet. (You can use a pencil to mark this onto the paper first if you like.) Pipe another smaller circle inside this one so you have two touching concentric circles. Pipe another ring on top of the two circles to give height to the rings. Brush the choux paste with the beaten egg yolk and scatter over the flaked/ slivered almonds, gently pressing them to adhere.

Bake in the preheated oven for 30–40 minutes until golden, risen and dry. The crust should be almost hollow inside; you will fill this with filling later.

To make the filling, combine the sugar with 90 ml/⅓ cup water in a small saucepan and boil until the sugar has dissolved and the temperature reaches 121°C (250°F) on a sugar thermometer. Remove from the heat and set aside.

Place the egg yolks and salt into the bowl of a stand mixer fitted with the paddle attachment (or use a hand-held electric whisk and large mixing bowl) and beat on medium speed until pale and fluffy. Very carefully drizzle the hot syrup over the yolks, mixing at low speed. The mixture will turn pale golden in colour and become fluffy and voluminous.

Slowly add the soft butter to the eggs, a cube at a time. Beat until all the butter has been combined, then turn the speed up to medium-high and beat until fluffy, light and smooth. Turn off the mixer and carefully fold through the almond butter, trying not to lose too much air. Spoon the filling into the second piping/pastry bag. Set aside until needed.

To assemble, use a serrated knife to carefully slice horizontally through the choux ring. Pipe blobs of the filling all the way around the bottom layer. Carefully sandwich the top layer on top and gently press down to seal. Refrigerate for 30 minutes to set slightly before dusting generously with icing/ confectioners' sugar to serve.

Millefeuille FRANCE

The French truly know how to create wonderful patisserie. We have taken a classic millefeuille recipe and turned it into an even more decadent and indulgent pastry with the addition of an intense and rich chocolate ganache.

100 g/¾ cup icing/confectioners' sugar, plus extra for dusting

320 g / 11 oz. ready-rolled all-butter puff pastry

600 g /1¼ lb/6 cups fresh raspberries

CRÈME LÉGÈRE

40 g/3¼ tablespoons caster/granulated sugar

175 ml/¾ cup full-fat/whole milk

1 teaspoon pure vanilla extract

2 egg yolks

20 g/2⅓ tablespoons plain/all-purpose flour, sifted

½ tablespoon cornflour/cornstarch, sifted

100 ml/½ cup double/heavy cream

FILLING

250 ml/1 cup double/heavy cream

15 g/1¾ tablespoons icing/confectioners' sugar

1 teaspoon pure vanilla extract

GANACHE

250 ml/1 cup double/heavy cream

100 g/3½ oz. dark/bittersweet chocolate (no more than 70% cocoa solids), chopped

100 g/3½ oz. milk chocolate, chopped

2 large baking sheets, 1 greased and lined with baking parchment.

2 piping/pastry bags fitted with 1-cm/½-inch plain nozzles/tips

MAKES 1 LARGE PASTRY

Dust the work surface liberally with icing/confectioners' sugar and roll out the pastry to a slightly bigger rectangle than the original ready-rolled pastry sheet. It should be as thin as you can get it without stretching the pastry. Place onto the lined baking sheet and sprinkle liberally with icing/confectioners' sugar. Chill for 30 minutes in the fridge. (You will trim the pastry once baked so no need to have straight edges at this stage.) Preheat the oven to 200°C (400°F) Gas 6.

Remove the pastry from the fridge and place the second baking sheet on top of the pastry to prevent the layers rising too much. Bake in the preheated oven for 15 minutes. Remove from the oven, remove the top baking sheet and sprinkle with more icing/confectioners' sugar. Set aside.

While the pastry is cooling, make the crème légère. Place three-quarters of the sugar into a saucepan with the milk and vanilla and heat until almost boiling. In another large bowl, beat the egg yolks with the remaining sugar until combined, then whisk in the flour and cornflour/cornstarch.

Slowly pour the hot milk over the egg mixture beating continuously. Pour back into the pan over medium heat and whisk continuously until thickened and simmering, about 5 minutes.

Pour into a large bowl and cover the surface with clingfilm/plastic wrap to stop a skin from forming. Refrigerate for at least 1 hour to set.

Once set, remove from the fridge and use a whisk to beat until smooth. In another bowl, whip the double/heavy cream to soft peaks. Slowly combine the cream with the custard and whisk until smooth and light. Refrigerate until needed.

For the filling, place the double/heavy cream, icing/confectioners' sugar and vanilla extract in a large bowl and whip until medium-stiff peaks form. This can be done by hand or with an electric whisk. Spoon the mixture into one of the piping/pastry bags and refrigerate until needed.

For the ganache, place the double/heavy cream into a small saucepan and heat until almost boiling. Remove from the heat and whisk in both types of chopped chocolate using a balloon whisk. Once smooth and glossy, scrape the ganache into a bowl. Refrigerate for a few hours or until the ganache is a spreadable consistency. Spoon the ganache into the second piping/pastry bag.

Take the cooled pastry sheet and very carefully use a serrated knife to trim the edges straight. Place the pastry with a long edge facing you and cut into three even shorter pieces. Use a ruler to help you if needed; the layers will need to be even in order to be stacked neatly.

Place one of the pastry layers onto a serving plate. Spread with a thin layer of crème légère. Pipe small blobs of cream filling along the pastry in three neat rows, leaving a row gap between them. Pipe blobs of ganache to fill in these gaps. Position raspberries on top of the cream in neat rows, then put another pastry layer on top and repeat the process. Top with the final layer of pastry and dust the top with icing/confectioners' sugar before serving.

Southern Europe

Sticky orange and almond cake SPAIN

Genoise sponge with raspberries ITALY

Chocolate and orange panettone ITALY

Torta di ricotta ITALY

Lemon polenta cake ITALY

Tiramisu cake ITALY

Vasilopita GREECE

Honey and orange cake GREECE

Lemon olive oil cake GREECE

Sticky orange and almond cake

SPAIN **GF** 🥄🥄

This is one of our absolute favourite cakes to serve at a dinner party. It is best to make ahead and store in the fridge, as this cake really does improve with age. By incorporating whole oranges into the batter, you gain a real bittersweet flavour, and blended with ground almonds, the resulting cake is moist and decadent. It is gluten-free too!

3 unwaxed seedless oranges

6 eggs

300 g/1½ cups caster/granulated sugar

250 g/2 cups ground almonds

1 teaspoon gluten-free baking powder

icing/confectioners' sugar, to decorate

crème fraiche and fresh raspberries, to serve (optional)

23-cm/9-inch round loose-bottom or springform cake pan, greased and lined with baking parchment

MAKES 1 LARGE CAKE

Preheat the oven to 180°C (350°F) Gas 4.

Start by placing your oranges in a pan and covering with water. Place the pan on the heat and boil the oranges for 40 minutes until they are soft to the touch. Drain and allow to cool, before placing the whole oranges into a blender or food processor and blending to a rough purée. You do not want the purée silky smooth, but you also do not want large chunks of orange flesh in it.

Place the eggs and sugar in a bowl and, using a balloon whisk, beat together until fully combined and frothy. Add the orange purée, ground almonds and baking powder and, using the whisk, mix all the ingredients together until fully combined.

Pour into the prepared cake pan and place in the centre of the oven to bake for 45 minutes, or until golden brown and a skewer inserted into the centre of the cake comes out clean

Allow to cool completely in the pan before running a sharp knife around the edge of the pan and releasing the cake. Place on a serving plate and lightly dust with icing/confectioners' sugar. Serve at room temperature with a spoonful of crème fraîche and some fresh raspberries, if you like, for a delicious dessert or teatime treat.

Genoise sponge with raspberries ITALY

This light and airy sponge cake hails from the Italian city of Genoa. Created with no chemical raising agents, the cake's incredible lightness comes solely from ultra-whipped eggs. Feel free to decorate your Genoise sponge as you choose, it is such a versatile recipe to master and gives endless opportunities to create delicious baked desserts.

30 g/¼ stick butter

6 eggs

200 g/1 cup caster/granulated sugar

160 g/scant 1¼ cups plain/all-purpose flour

25 g/⅛ cup cornflour/cornstarch

250 ml/1 cup double/heavy cream, softly whipped

400 g/14 oz. fresh raspberries

icing/confectioners' sugar, to dust

23-cm/9-inch round loose-bottom or springform cake pan, greased and lined with baking parchment

MAKES 1 LARGE CAKE

Preheat the oven to 160°C (325°F) Gas 3.

Melt the butter and set aside to cool. Place the eggs and the sugar into the bowl of a stand mixer fitted with a whisk attachment (or use a hand-held electric whisk and large mixing bowl) and beat together on a high speed until trebled in size and a light and creamy colour. This will take about 5 minutes.

Carefully sift the flour and cornflour/cornstarch onto the egg mixture and slowly fold in using a metal spoon to combine. Gently fold through the melted butter – you do not want to lose all the air that you have whisked into the eggs at this point, so take your time to combine everything.

Pour the mixture carefully into the prepared cake pan and bake in the centre of the preheated oven for 35 minutes or until well risen, golden and springy to the touch.

Allow to cool in the pan for 10 minutes, then slowly run a knife around the edge of the pan to release the cake. Turn it onto a wire rack to cool completely and remove the baking parchment while still warm.

Using a serrated knife, slice horizontally through the middle of the sponge to create two even layers. Spoon the whipped cream onto the bottom layer of the sponge and arrange half of the raspberries in a circular pattern. Place the other layer of the sponge on top, then decorate with the remaining raspberries. Lightly dust with icing/confectioners' sugar.

Serve straightaway with a cup of tea or glass of champagne if you wish – delicious!

Panettone: Toni's cake

Hailing from Milan, panettone is a sweet bread, enjoyed around the world at Christmas and New Year. Usually given as a gift, presented or sold in luxurious looking boxes tied up with shiny ribbon, it is the perfect celebration cake for festive times of the year. Though the store-bought version is easy to find, it is so rewarding to make this treat at home and let the fragrance of warm, sweet dough fill your kitchen.

There are many fanciful Italian stories over how the recipe originated or got its name. Featuring a cast of different Toni's that the bread 'Pan di Toni' (Toni's Cake) was named after. An alternative theory is that the bread is not named after a person at all, but rather can be translated in Milanese as 'bread of luxury'. Yet a third theory is that panettone started life as a little loaf ('panetto') before being re-made as panettone 'little big loaf'.

Primitive versions of the recipe are thought to have been around since Roman times, when it was sweetened with honey and shaped flat like a focaccia before modern raising agents existed. Taller versions started appearing along with the invention of baking powder in the 1850s. In the 19th century, Angelo Motta, an Italian baking entrepreneur, was the first to produce the classic domed shape on an industrial scale, setting the standard for the panettone we all know.

Traditionally, the bread is made with a sourdough starter and left to rise three times. Our more attainable but still delicious version allows for two rises and uses dried yeast. Flavour additions include dried fruits, citrus, rum or chocolate. You can eat panettone warm as a dessert paired with cream, cold with a glass of mulled wine, or even toasted for breakfast with coffee.

Chocolate and orange panettone ITALY

There is nothing like the smell of freshly baked bread…well, actually there is! The smell of fresh panettone in your kitchen is just incredible. We have taken a classic recipe and added one of our favourite flavour combinations to create this Italian treat. Great at festive times as well as all year round, it's worth the effort, and watching the enriched dough rise is a cathartic experience. Read more about panettone on the opposite page.

4 tablespoons warm milk

15 g/½ oz. active dried yeast

100 g/½ cup caster/granulated sugar

250 g/2¼ sticks butter

2 teaspoons pure vanilla extract

grated zest of 2 oranges

5 eggs

500 g/3½ cups white strong/bread flour, plus a little extra for dusting

pinch of salt

100 g/3½ oz. good-quality dark/bittersweet chocolate, chopped

icing/confectioners' sugar, to decorate

23-cm/9-inch round loose-bottom or springform cake pan or panettone pan, greased and lined with baking parchment

MAKES 1 LARGE PANETTONE

Place the warm milk in a bowl and add the yeast and 1 teaspoon of the sugar. Stir to dissolve, then leave for 5 minutes to go bubbly.

Put the remaining sugar into the bowl of a stand mixer fitted with the paddle attachment (or use a hand-held electric whisk and large mixing bowl) along with the butter and vanilla extract and beat until really light, creamy and pale. Stir in the orange zest. Add the eggs, one at a time, beating until well combined. Stir in the yeast mixture.

Add the flour and salt, folding in with a large spoon to make a soft dough. Knead for 5 minutes using the dough hook attachment or in the mixing bowl using your hands (oil your hands to avoid too much stickiness) until it all starts to come together. It will be a sticky dough at this stage.

If you are using your hands, turn out the dough onto a floured surface and knead for a further 10 minutes; if using a stand mixer, knead for 5 minutes on medium speed until everything has come together and you have a very soft and stretchy dough. (If kneading by hand, add a light sprinkling of flour to the surface and your hands as you go to stop the mixture sticking, but try not to add too much.)

Place in a lightly oiled bowl and cover with clingfilm/plastic wrap. Leave in a warm place for 2 hours or until doubled in size.

When the dough has risen, tip it out onto a lightly floured surface and knead for another 5 minutes. Gradually knead in the chopped chocolate. Shape the dough into a ball and place into the prepared cake pan. (If using a loose-bottom or springform cake pan, wrap a layer of baking parchment around the outside of the pan, to come up about 5 cm/2 inches above the rim, and secure the paper with string. This will help contain the dough as it rises up.) Cover lightly with cling film/plastic wrap and leave to rise for another hour or until it has risen to the top of the pan or paper.

Preheat the oven to 180°C (350°F) Gas 4.

Adjust the oven shelf to the right height to accommodate the pan. Place in the centre of the preheated oven and bake for 40–50 minutes until golden and risen and a skewer inserted into the centre of the panettone comes out clean. Leave to cool in the pan for 10 minutes before turning out onto a wire rack. Leave to cool completely before dusting lightly with icing/confectioners' sugar and serving.

Torta di ricotta ITALY 🥄

A truly delicious cake. There are strong similarities between this cake and a baked cheesecake, however, we love the lightness and the simplicity of this torta. Scented with citrus and fluffy like a cloud, we don't think you can go wrong with our take on this classic.

680 g/1½ lb. ricotta cheese, blended until smooth in a mixer or with a whisk

6 eggs, separated

35 g/¼ cup plain/all-purpose flour, sifted

200 g/1 cup caster/granulated sugar

grated zest of 2 oranges

grated zest of 1 lemon

pinch of salt

icing/confectioners' sugar, to dust

23-cm/9-inch round loose-bottom or springform cake pan, greased with butter and sprinkled with sugar

MAKES 1 LARGE TORTA

Preheat the oven to 180°C (350°F) Gas 4.

Place the ricotta, egg yolks, flour, 6 tablespoons of the sugar, the orange and lemon zests, and the salt into the bowl of a stand mixer fitted with the whisk attachment (or use a hand-held electric whisk and large mixing bowl) and whisk to combine.

In a separate bowl, whisk the egg whites on low speed until foamy. Increase the speed to high and gradually add the remaining sugar, whisking until stiff, glossy peaks form; this may take up to 3–4 minutes.

Gently fold one-third of the whites into the ricotta mixture using a spatula until just combined. Gently fold in the remaining whites until just combined. Pour the mixture carefully into the prepared cake pan and bake in the preheated oven for 50–60 minutes or until the centre is firm and the top is a deep golden brown. The mixture will rise up and then drop down slightly during cooking.

Allow to cool in the pan on a wire rack for 10 minutes. Run a knife around the edge of the cake to release it from the pan, then turn it out and allow to cool completely before serving dusted with plenty of icing/confectioners' sugar.

Lemon polenta cake

ITALY GF 🥄

This gluten-free cake has a delightful texture with a real zing from the lemon syrup it's soaked in. To add to the atmosphere, try teaming your cake with a chilled glass of Italian limoncello.

200 g/1¾ sticks butter, softened

200 g/1 cup golden caster/granulated sugar

200 g/2 cups ground almonds

100 g/⅔ cup polenta or fine cornmeal

1½ teaspoons baking powder

3 eggs

grated zest of 3 unwaxed lemons

SYRUP

freshly squeezed juice of 2 lemons

125 g/¾ cup plus 2 tablespoons sifted icing/confectioners' sugar

23-cm/9-inch round loose-bottom or springform cake pan, greased and base-lined with baking parchment

MAKES 1 LARGE CAKE

Preheat the oven to 180°C (350°F) Gas 4.

Place the butter and sugar into the bowl of a stand mixer fitted with a paddle attachment (or use a wooden spoon and large mixing bowl) and beat until pale and fluffy. Mix together the almonds, polenta or fine cornmeal and baking powder, then beat some of this into the butter and sugar mixture, followed by 1 egg. Continue adding the remaining dry ingredients and eggs in this way, beating after each addition. Finally, beat in the lemon zest.

Spoon the mixture into the prepared cake pan and bake in the preheated oven for 40–45 minutes or until a skewer inserted into the centre of the cake comes out clean. Remove the cake from the oven and allow to cool in the pan.

Meanwhile, make the syrup by heating the lemon juice and icing/confectioners' sugar together in a small pan. Once the sugar has dissolved into the juice, remove from the heat and set aside.

Prick the top of the cake all over with a cocktail stick/toothpick and pour the warm syrup over the cake. Allow to cool before removing it from the pan and serving.

Tiramisù cake ITALY 🥄🥄🥄

We have reimagined the classic Italian dessert into this magnificent show-stopper. Chocolate sponges are soaked with a brandy and coffee syrup, layered with creamy mascarpone frosting and finished with lashings of dark chocolate.

75 g/¾ stick butter

6 eggs

210 g/1 cup caster/granulated sugar

2 teaspoons pure vanilla extract

150 g/1 cup plus 2 tablespoons plain/all-purpose flour

40 g/scant ½ cup unsweetened cocoa powder

¾ teaspoon baking powder

pinch of salt

FROSTING

250 g/9 oz. full-fat cream cheese

450 g/1 lb. mascarpone

150 g/1 cup icing/confectioners' sugar, sifted

2 teaspoons instant espresso powder

SYRUP

1 tablespoon instant espresso powder

2 tablespoons soft light brown sugar

150 ml/⅔ cup boiling water

100 ml/⅓ cup brandy

TO DECORATE

unsweetened cocoa powder

50 g/2 oz. dark/bittersweet chocolate, very finely chopped

2 x 23-cm/9-inch round loose-bottom or springform cake pans, greased and lined with baking parchment

MAKES 1 LARGE CAKE

Preheat the oven to 180°C (350°F) Gas 4.

Melt the butter and set aside to cool. Place the eggs, sugar and vanilla extract into the bowl of a stand mixer fitted with the whisk attachment (or use a hand-held electric whisk and large mixing bowl) and whisk for about 6 minutes or until the mixture is pale, thick and has trebled in volume.

Sift the flour, cocoa powder, baking powder and salt over the egg mixture, then fold together using a spatula. Pour the cooled melted butter into the mixture and mix gently until fully incorporated.

Divide the batter between the prepared cake pans and bake in the preheated oven for 15–18 minutes or until a skewer inserted into the centre comes out clean. Cool in the pans for a few minutes, then transfer to a wire rack to cool fully.

Use a serrated knife to slice each cake in half horizontally to create four even layers. Set aside.

To make the frosting, combine the cream cheese, mascarpone cheese, icing/confectioners' sugar and espresso powder in the bowl of a stand mixer fitted with the paddle attachment (or use a hand-held electric whisk and large mixing bowl) and beat on high speed for a minute or so until well combined, light and fluffy. Set aside.

To make the syrup, dissolve the instant espresso powder and brown sugar in the boiling water and stir in the brandy. Set aside to cool. The liquid will be very runny and will not thicken.

To assemble the cake, line the whole of the inside of one of your cake pans with clingfilm/plastic wrap, leaving no gaps. Insert one of the sponges and sprinkle with the syrup. Allow to soak in and gently press down. Take a quarter of the frosting and spread over the sponge. Repeat the process with the remaining three sponges, using all the syrup and finishing with the frosting on top.

Dust the cake with cocoa powder and sprinkle with chopped chocolate. Cover the cake with clingfilm/plastic wrap and refrigerate for at least 4 hours or ideally overnight. To remove the cake, undo the spring of the pan and peel the clingfilm/plastic wrap away from the cake. Place on a serving plate and enjoy.

A traditional tavern in the village of Makrinitsa, Greece (left).

Freshly picked almonds and ripe citrus fruit, sunshine baking at its best (above left and right).

Italian's love their coffee! A waiter carries a tray of espressos in the Tuscany region of Italy (right).

A cake to welcome Pope Francis is displayed in the window of a café in Florence, Italy (left).

The historic Forn des Teatre bakery in Mallorca, Spain (right).

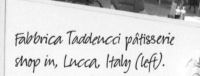

Fabbrica Taddeucci pâtisserie shop in, Lucca, Italy (left).

Amor di cioccolato

Vasilopita GREECE

This is our take on a traditional cake served in the New Year in Greece. It is strewn with sticky caramelized almonds and honey, and a hidden layer of almonds then runs through the centre. Serve with a strong cup of coffee on New Year's day!

100 g/1¼ cups flaked/slivered almonds

60 g/⅓ cup minus 1 tablespoon soft light brown sugar

1 tablespoon runny honey, plus extra to serve

450 g/scant 3½ cups plain/all-purpose flour, sifted

2 teaspoons baking powder

½ teaspoon bicarbonate of soda/baking soda

250 g/2¼ sticks butter, softened

450 g/2¼ cups caster/granulated sugar

6 eggs

grated zest of 1 orange or satsuma

2 teaspoons freshly squeezed lemon juice

1 teaspoon pure vanilla extract

230 ml/scant 1 cup full-fat/whole milk

10-cm/4-inch loose-bottom or springform cake pan, greased and lined with baking parchment

23-cm/9-inch loose-bottom or springform cake pan, greased and lined with baking parchment

MAKES 1 LARGE CAKE

Preheat the oven to 160°C (325°F) Gas 3.

Mix together the almonds, brown sugar and honey in a small bowl. Set aside.

Mix together the flour, baking powder and bicarbonate of soda/baking soda in a medium bowl. Set aside.

Place the butter and sugar into the bowl of a stand mixer fitted with the paddle attachment (or use a hand-held electric whisk and large mixing bowl) and beat on medium speed until light and fluffy.

Add the eggs, one at a time, beating well after each addition. Stir in the orange zest, lemon juice and vanilla. Add the flour mixture a little at a time, alternating with the milk, and mix well.

To assemble the cake, divide one-third of the honey and almond mixture between the two prepared cake pans, spreading it in an even layer over their bases. Fill the smaller pan half-full of batter, and then spoon half of the remaining batter into the larger pan. Bake both layers in the preheated oven for 30 minutes, until the cakes are partially cooked.

Sprinkle the remaining honey and almond mixture in an even layer over the partially baked cakes. Spoon the remaining batter on top of each cake. Bake for a further 20 minutes for the small cake and 40–45 minutes for the large cake or until a skewer inserted into the centre of each cake comes out clean. Allow the cakes to cool in their pans for 10 minutes.

To assemble the cake, carefully run a knife around the edge of each cake pan and invert the large cake onto a serving plate, scraping any of the sticky nuts from the pan and placing on the top. Allow to cool before placing the inverted smaller cake on top to create a second tier. Drizzle with some honey to serve.

Honey and orange cake GREECE GF 🥄

This wonderful gluten-free cake is fragrant with orange and sticky with honey. Teamed with some sunshine you could almost be transported to the Greek islands! Depending on the honey you choose, this cake can be light and fragrant or dark and woody. This is entirely your preference – we like to use a floral yet mild honey.

CAKE

3 small oranges (approx. weight 250 g/9 oz.)

125 g/1¼ cups ground almonds

175 g/1½ sticks butter

175 g/¾ cup plus 2 tablespoons golden caster/granulated sugar

3 eggs, beaten

250 g/1⅔ cups polenta or fine cornmeal

4½ teaspoons baking powder

HONEY SYRUP

225 ml/scant 1 cup Greek honey

5 tablespoons freshly squeezed orange juice

1½ tablespoons freshly squeezed lemon juice

TOPPING

200 g/7 oz. thick Greek yogurt

2 tablespoons Greek honey

40 g/¼ cup unsalted, shelled pistachio nuts

23-cm/9-inch round loose-bottom or springform cake pan, greased and lined with baking parchment

MAKES 1 LARGE CAKE

Preheat the oven to 200°C (400°F) Gas 6.

Cut the oranges into pieces (without peeling) and carefully remove any pips you see. Place the oranges into a blender or food processor and purée until smooth, skin and all. Place the remaining cake ingredients into the bowl of a stand mixer fitted with a paddle attachment (or use a hand-held electric whisk and large mixing bowl) and beat together on medium speed until smooth. Add the orange purée and mix until fully combined. Spoon the mixture into the prepared cake pan and bake in the preheated oven for 45–55 minutes or until golden brown and a skewer inserted into the centre of the cake comes out clean. Allow to cool in the pan while you make the syrup.

For the syrup, place the honey, orange juice and lemon juice into a small saucepan and simmer gently over low heat for 5 minutes until slightly reduced.

Carefully remove the slightly cooled cake from the pan and place onto a wire rack with a large baking sheet underneath. Use a cocktail stick/toothpick to prick the cake all over and then carefully drizzle the honey syrup over the surface of the cake. The baking sheet underneath the rack will catch any drips (which can then be poured back over the cake once cool). Use all the syrup and then allow to cool completely.

For the topping, casually swirl the Greek yogurt over the surface of the cooled cake, drizzle with the honey and scatter over the pistachio nuts. Any syrup left on the baking sheet under the cake can also be drizzled over the surface.

Lemon olive oil cake

GREECE DF 🥄

2 large lemons

125 g/1 cup minus
1 tablespoon plain/
all-purpose flour, sifted

5 egg yolks and 4 egg
whites

220 g/1 cup plus 1½
tablespoons caster/
granulated sugar

180 ml/¾ cup olive oil

½ teaspoon salt

DECORATION

250 g/1¾ cups icing/
confectioners' sugar,
sifted

2 tablespoons freshly
squeezed lemon juice

grated zest of 1 lemon

*23-cm/9-inch round
loose-bottom or
springform cake pan,
greased and lined with
baking parchment*

MAKES 1 LARGE CAKE

This dairy-free cake is a summery delight. Zingy with citrus and light as a feather, it really is a taste of holidays past. Enjoy with a digestif after dinner for a wonderful end to an evening.

Preheat the oven to 180°C (350°F) Gas 4.

Finely grate the zest from both lemons and mix together with the flour. Halve one of the lemons and squeeze the juice into a small bowl. Place the egg yolks and 150 g/¾ cup of the sugar into the bowl of a stand mixer fitted with a whisk attachment (or use a hand-held electric whisk and large mixing bowl) and beat on high speed until thick and pale, about 3 minutes. Reduce the speed to medium and add the olive oil and 2 tablespoons of the squeezed lemon juice, beating until just combined (the mixture may appear separated). Use a spatula to stir in the flour mixture until just combined.

Place the egg whites and the salt into another large, grease-free mixing bowl. Make sure the whisk is completely clean, then whisk on medium-high speed using a hand-held electric whisk until foamy. Add the remaining sugar gradually, whisking continuously until the egg whites form soft peaks, about 3 minutes. Gently fold one-third of the whites into the yolk mixture, before folding in the remaining whites thoroughly.

Spoon the batter into the prepared cake pan and gently tap against the work surface to release any air bubbles. Bake in the preheated oven for 40–50 minutes or until golden and a skewer inserted into the centre of the cake comes out clean. Cool the cake in the pan for 10 minutes, then place on a wire rack to cool completely. Once cool transfer to a serving plate. To decorate, place the icing/confectioners' sugar into a bowl and mix in the lemon juice using a hand whisk or fork until it's a pouring consistency similar to double/heavy cream. Gently pour over the cake, allowing it to drizzle down the sides.

Sprinkle with grated lemon zest and serve.

The Middle East and Africa

Mosaic cake TURKEY

Fig and sesame cake TURKEY

Chocolate tahini cake LEBANON

Honey cake ISRAEL

Pomegranate cake IRAN

Date and spice cake IRAQ

Baklava cake SAUDI ARABIA

Snake cake MOROCCO

Fig and pumpkin cake TUNISIA

Amarula cake SOUTH AFRICA

Peanut and banana cake GHANA

Mosaic cake TURKEY

It seems that many countries have their own spin on what is known as a 'refrigerator cake'. This wonderful Turkish cake is a great example of one such cake. Set in the fridge with no baking required, this is a fun recipe to make with children for a real chocolate treat. Feel free to customize your cake with whatever nuts and dried fruits you have handy.

250 g/2¼ sticks butter

250 g/1¼ cups caster/granulated sugar

4 tablespoons unsweetened cocoa powder, sifted

2 eggs

500 g/1 lb. 2 oz. digestive biscuits/graham crackers (ginger nut/snap biscuits also work well)

180 g/1½ cups chopped nuts (we like flaked/slivered almonds or pistachios)

150 g/1 cup dried apricots, chopped (also works well with dried cherries)

icing/confectioners' sugar, to dust

MAKES 1 LARGE CAKE

Start by melting the butter and sugar together in a pan until the sugar has dissolved; this should take 5–10 minutes. Remove from the heat, add the cocoa powder and mix well. Once the mixture has cooled a little, add the eggs and mix again until fully combined and thickened. Finally, break the digestive biscuits/graham crackers into chunks and add them with the nuts and dried fruit, mixing well.

Lay some clingfilm/plastic wrap on a baking sheet. Pour the mixture onto the clingfilm/plastic wrap, then roll into a fat sausage. Put the cake into the fridge for 2 hours until set. Unwrap the roll, dust all over with icing/confectioners' sugar and serve cold, cut into slices.

Fig and sesame cake TURKEY **GF** 🥄🥄

We adore figs here at Lola's and our favourite are the plump and sweet purple Turkish figs. With the addition of sesame seeds and dried figs, this naturally gluten-free cake has a wonderful texture and is very pretty to serve on an afternoon tea plate. Alternatively, serve it with an authentic Turkish coffee. Either warm or cold, this cake will definitely transport you to the streets of Istanbul.

Preheat the oven to 180°C (350°F) Gas 4.

Sprinkle the sides of the prepared cake pan with the sesame seeds. Where you have greased the pan, the sesame seeds should adhere to the sides. Slice each fig in half vertically and carefully arrange in the base of the pan to form a pretty pattern. (You will see the figs as the cake will be inverted.) Melt the butter gently and set aside.

Place the ground almonds, polenta or fine cornmeal, icing/confectioners' sugar and orange zest into a large mixing bowl. Add the egg yolks and melted butter. Beat with a wooden spoon – the batter will be pretty stiff.

Place the egg whites in a separate clean, grease-free bowl and using an electric hand-held whisk (or in a stand mixer fitted with the whisk attachment) whisk on medium speed until soft peaks form, about 3 minutes. Add one large spoonful of the whisked egg whites to the cake batter to loosen the mixture, before folding in the remaining egg whites until fully incorporated. Fold in the chopped dried figs.

Carefully spoon the batter over the figs in the pan and bake in the centre of the preheated oven for 50–60 minutes or until a skewer inserted into the centre of the cake comes out clean.

Meanwhile, make the syrup by placing the honey and 3 tablespoons of water into a small pan. Bring to the boil, then remove from the heat and set aside.

Remove the cooked cake from the oven and, using a cocktail stick/toothpick, prick it all over before slowly drizzling the syrup over the warm cake. Allow to cool completely in the pan before inverting the cake onto a serving plate.

15 g/2 tablespoons sesame seeds

7 fresh black figs

50 g/3½ tablespoons butter

200 g/2 cups ground almonds

85 g/½ cup polenta or fine cornmeal

140 g/1 cup icing/confectioners' sugar, sifted

grated zest of 1 orange

5 eggs, separated

150 g/1 cup dried figs, chopped

SYRUP

150 g/¾ cup honey of your choice

23-cm/9-inch round loose-bottom or springform cake pan, greased and base-lined with baking parchment

MAKES 1 LARGE CAKE

Chocolate tahini cake LEBANON DF 🥄

This delightful and ridiculously simple cake is a real treat. Combining the nuttiness of sesame with the richness of chocolate we have created a dairy-, egg-, and refined sugar-free cake. Who'd have thought that tahini could be used in such a creative way? We give thanks to our Lebanese friends for giving us the inspiration to use this wonderful ingredient.

60g/½ cup plus 1 tablespoon good-quality unsweetened cocoa powder

270 g/2 cups plain/all-purpose flour, sifted

2 teaspoons baking powder

1 teaspoon bicarbonate of soda/baking soda

pinch of salt

295 g/1¼ cups smooth tahini

225 g/⅔ cup runny honey

1 large ripe banana, mashed with a fork

1 teaspoon pure vanilla extract

270 ml/1¼ scant cups almond or soy milk

TO DECORATE

1 tablespoon runny honey

1 teaspoon toasted sesame seeds

23-cm/9-inch round loose-bottom or springform cake pan, greased and lined with baking parchment

MAKES 1 LARGE CAKE

Preheat the oven to 180°C (350°F) Gas 4.

In a large bowl, sift together the cocoa powder, flour, baking powder, bicarbonate of soda/baking soda and salt. Set aside. In another bowl, mix the tahini, honey, mashed banana, vanilla and milk.

Slowly pour the wet ingredients into the dry ingredients and, using a wooden spoon, beat together until fully incorporated.

Spoon the batter into the prepared cake pan and bake in the preheated oven for 40–50 minutes or until risen and a skewer inserted into the centre of the cake comes out clean.

Allow the cake to cool completely in the pan. When ready to serve, release the cake from its pan and place on a serving plate. Drizzle the runny honey over the cake and sprinkle with the sesame seeds to decorate. Delicious enjoyed with a strong Middle Eastern-style coffee.

Honey cake ISRAEL

This moist and fragrant cake is inspired by our travels through Istanbul and Turkey. We are huge honey fans and make it our duty to taste as many types as we can while we are abroad. This cake works well with strong, rich varieties of honey which give a deep, dark flavour. By adding a little spice and some nuts we think we have made the perfect dessert to end any Middle Eastern feast.

125 g/1 cup minus 1 tablespoon plain/all-purpose flour, sifted

1½ teaspoons bicarbonate of soda/baking soda

¼ teaspoon ground ginger

¼ teaspoon ground nutmeg

pinch of salt

½ teaspoon ground cinnamon

grated zest of 1 orange

170 g/1½ sticks butter, softened

150 g/¾ cup caster/granulated sugar

3 eggs

60 ml/¼ cup milk

1 tablespoon runny honey, plus extra to decorate

1 ripe banana, mashed with a fork

80 g/¾ cup chopped walnuts

sugar bees or fresh flowers, to decorate

SYRUP

100 g/½ cup caster/granulated sugar

175 g/½ cup runny honey

1 teaspoon pomegranate molasses

26-cm/10½-inch Bundt pan or decorative ring mould, greased and floured

MAKES 1 LARGE CAKE

Preheat the oven to 160°C (325°F) Gas 3.

Place the flour, bicarbonate of soda/baking soda, ginger, nutmeg, salt, cinnamon and orange zest into a large bowl and set aside.

Place the butter and sugar into the bowl of a stand mixer fitted with the paddle attachment (or use a hand-held electric whisk and large mixing bowl) and beat together on medium speed until they are nice and fluffy. Beat in the eggs, one at a time, along with the milk, alternating between the two and stopping to scrape down the sides of the bowl occasionally.

Add the honey and banana to the mix and beat well. Carefully add the dry ingredients to the wet ingredients and mix until fully combined. Fold in the chopped walnuts.

Pour the mixture into the prepared cake pan or mould and bake in the preheated oven for 40–50 minutes until a skewer inserted into the thickest part of the cake comes out clean. Allow the cake to cool in the pan or mould.

Meanwhile, place all the ingredients for the syrup along with 80 ml/⅓ cup water into a small pan over medium heat. Bring to the boil and cook for 3 minutes, stirring occasionally.

Pierce the cake all over with a skewer and carefully drizzle some of the syrup all over. Leave it to sink in for a minute or two, then pour the rest over the cake until it is all covered. Allow to sit for an hour or so to absorb all of the syrup, and then remove the cake from the pan. Decorate with a generous extra drizzle of runny honey.

Pomegranate cake IRAN 🥄

We love the jewel-bright colour of pomegranate seeds; they are evocative of treasures and exotic climates. This fluffy sponge is flavoured with both pomegranate molasses and seeds. It is topped with a light cream cheese frosting and scattered with yet more beautiful ruby-red seeds to finish.

200 g/1¾ sticks butter, softened

200 g/1 cup caster/granulated sugar

3 eggs

1 teaspoon pure vanilla extract

grated zest and freshly squeezed juice of ½ lemon

240 g self-raising flour/1¾ cups cake flour mixed with 4 teaspoons baking powder, sifted

1 tablespoon pomegranate molasses

50 g/⅓ cup fresh pomegranate seeds

SYRUP

1 tablespoon pomegranate molasses

freshly squeezed juice of ½ lemon

80 g/scant ½ cup caster/granulated sugar

½ teaspoon pure vanilla extract

150 g/1 cup fresh pomegranate seeds

FROSTING

250 g/1¼ cups full-fat cream cheese

50 ml /¼ cup double/heavy cream

80 g/½ cup icing/confectioners' sugar

23-cm/9-inch round loose-bottom or springform cake pan, greased and lined with baking parchment

MAKES 1 LARGE CAKE

Preheat the oven to 160°C (325°F) Gas 3.

Place the butter and sugar into the bowl of a stand mixer fitted with the paddle attachment (or use a hand-held electric whisk and large mixing bowl) and beat on medium speed until fluffy and fully mixed.

With the speed set on slow, add the eggs, one at a time, stopping to scrape down the sides of the bowl as you go. Add the vanilla extract, lemon zest and juice and the flour and blend slowly until just mixed. Add the pomegranate molasses and pomegranate seeds and carefully mix until just combined.

Spoon the cake batter into the prepared cake pan and smooth the surface level. Bake in the preheated oven for 45–50 minutes until risen and a skewer inserted into the centre of the cake comes out clean. Allow to cool in the pan slightly while you make the syrup.

For the syrup, place all the ingredients except the pomegranate seeds into a small pan along with 80 ml/⅓ cup water. Heat gently until the sugar has melted. Turn the heat to high and boil for 5 minutes until slightly syrupy. Spoon half of the warm syrup over the warm cake and set aside to cool completely in the pan. Add the fresh pomegranate seeds to the remaining syrup and set aside to cool fully.

For the frosting, place all the ingredients into a large bowl and beat by hand using a balloon whisk or using an hand-held electric whisk until thick and creamy. This will take a few minutes.

Turn out the cool cake onto a serving plate. Spoon over the cream cheese frosting and use a palette knife or metal spatula to smooth it to the edges in a rustic style. Carefully spoon the remaining syrup and seeds over the frosting and allow it to drip down the sides of the cake. Slice and enjoy!

Date and spice cake

IRAQ

This lovely cake takes inspiration from the Middle East and the abundance of spices and dried fruits available in most souks. Perfect for the cooler months served with custard or ice cream!

380 g/2½ cups dried pitted dates, chopped

300 ml/1¼ cups warm water

¼ teaspoon bicarbonate of soda/baking soda

225 g self-raising flour/1¾ cups cake flour mixed with 4 teaspoons baking powder

pinch of salt

½ teaspoon ground cinnamon

⅛ teaspoon ground cloves

¼ teaspoon ground ginger

⅛ teaspoon ground nutmeg

200 g/1 cup soft light brown sugar

90 g/¾ stick butter, softened

3 eggs

1 teaspoon pure vanilla extract

GLAZE

75 g/¾ stick butter, softened

50 g/¼ cup soft light brown sugar

2 tablespoons full-fat/whole milk, plus extra if needed

½ teaspoon pure vanilla extract

125 g/¾ cup plus 2 tablespoons icing/confectioners' sugar, sifted

TO DECORATE:

20 g/1 oz. dried dates, chopped

26-cm/10½-inch Bundt pan or decorative ring mould, greased and floured

MAKES 1 LARGE CAKE

Preheat the oven to 180°C (350°F) Gas 4.

Start by placing the chopped dates and water into a small saucepan and set over low heat. Bring to the boil and then immediately remove from the heat before adding the bicarbonate of soda/baking soda. Stir and set aside to cool slightly before placing into a blender or food processor and blending to a rough paste.

Sift the flour, salt and all the spices together into a large mixing bowl. Set aside. Place the sugar and butter into the bowl of a stand mixer fitted with the paddle attachment (or use a hand-held electric whisk and large mixing bowl) and beat on medium speed until light and fluffy; this should take a couple of minutes.

Carefully add the eggs, one at a time, stopping after each addition to scrape down the sides of the bowl. Add the vanilla extract and the blended date mixture and mix well.

Once combined, add the sifted dry ingredients and beat until you have a smooth batter. Do not overmix at this stage. Pour the batter into the prepared cake pan and bake in the centre of the preheated oven for 45–55 minutes until well risen and a skewer inserted into the centre of the cake comes out clean.

Allow the cake to cool completely in the pan or mould. When ready to serve, release the cake from the pan and place onto a serving plate.

To make the glaze, place the butter, brown sugar, milk and vanilla extract into a heavy-bottomed saucepan and bring to the boil. Once the sugar has dissolved and you have a smooth sauce, remove from the heat and slowly whisk in the icing/confectioners' sugar. You can do this by hand, but be careful as the mixture will be very hot. If you find the glaze is too stiff, add a little extra milk to loosen the mixture.

Once the glaze has cooled slightly, pour it over the cake and allow the glaze to drizzle down the sides. Finish by scattering over the chopped dates to decorate, if you like.

Baklava cake SAUDI ARABIA

Inspired by sticky baklava, this gorgeous cake is our baker Julia's favourite recipe. Turn to pages 106–107 to read more about this Middle Eastern delicacy.

270-g/10-oz packet of filo/phyllo pastry

100 g/1 stick minus 1 tablespoon butter, melted

100 g/1 cup shelled pistachio nuts, toasted and ground

SYRUP

225 g/1 cup plus 2 tablespoons caster/granulated sugar

75 g/¼ cup runny honey

2 teaspoons pomegranate molasses

½ teaspoon rose water

¾ teaspoon orange flower water

CAKE

70 g/¾ cup panko or regular white breadcrumbs

100 g/1 cup ground almonds

80 g/¾ cup shelled pistachio nuts, roasted

2 teaspoons baking powder

1 teaspoon ground cinnamon

¼ teaspoon grated nutmeg

170 g/¾ cup plus 1½ tablespoons caster/granulated sugar

110 g/1 stick butter, softened

4 eggs

3 x 23-cm/9-inch round loose-bottom or springform cake pans, greased and lined with baking parchment

MAKES 1 LARGE CAKE

Preheat the oven to 180°C (350°F) Gas 4.

Make the syrup. Combine the sugar, honey, pomegranate molasses and 175 ml/¾ cup water in a heavy-bottomed saucepan over medium heat. Bring to the boil, then reduce the heat and simmer for 5 minutes until syrupy. Remove from the heat and stir in the rose and orange flower waters. Set aside to cool.

Next, make the cake. Combine the breadcrumbs, ground almonds, pistachios, baking powder, cinnamon and nutmeg in a small food processor. Process the ingredients to a medium/fine powder. Set aside.

Put the sugar and butter into the bowl of a stand mixer fitted with the paddle attachment (or use a hand-held electric whisk and large mixing bowl) and beat on medium speed until light and fluffy. Beat in the eggs, one at a time, stopping to scrape down the sides of the bowl as you go. Add the dry ingredients and mix until combined, being careful not to over-mix the batter.

Pour the batter into one of the prepared cake pans and bake in the preheated oven for 30–40 minutes, until a skewer inserted comes out clean. Leave the oven on. Brush the cake generously with syrup and let it cool in the pan. Slice the cold cake in half with a serrated knife.

To create the pastry layers, cut out 14 circles, roughly 5 cm/2 inches wider than the cake pan. Divide the circles into two piles of seven and cover with a damp kitchen towel to prevent them drying out.

Place one sheet of pastry in one of the prepared cake pans and fold in the edges to fit. Brush with melted butter. Repeat until you have four layers of buttered pastry. Scatter over one-third of the ground pistachios and continue layering and buttering three more layers. Repeat this process with the second pan, then brush the tops of both with melted butter.

Bake both pans of layered pastry in the preheated oven for 30–35 minutes until golden and crisp on top. Remove from the oven and drizzle 60 ml/¼ cup of the syrup into each pan. Set aside to cool completely, then carefully remove from the pans.

To assemble the cake, place one half of the cake onto a plate and brush with syrup. Add a pastry layer and brush with more syrup. Repeat the process, finishing with the second pastry layer on top. Drizzle over the remaining syrup and scatter with the last third of pistachios to finish. Allow to sit for at least an hour before serving.

Baklava: the queen of sweets

These sticky, exotic diamond parcels of rich, nutty goodness are famous for their moreish allure. Also known as Baghlava, Farsi for 'many leaves', this delicious treat is a favourite of Persian, Greek, Turkish and Saudi Arabian cuisine, among others. Modern recipes are the result of an amazing fusion of Middle Eastern cultures and beyond, each bringing their own subtle adaptation to the dish.

Baklava is normally made with filo/phyllo pastry, which is layered with chopped nuts and melted butter. The pastry is baked in a large tray until golden and crisp, then soaked in a fragrant syrup (made with sugar or honey) before being sliced into diamonds or squares. We have incorporated our favourite version of baklava into a wonderful cake, which manages to spread the delicious components out over several mouthfuls, rather than one brief, intense sugar-filled bite. Baklava can be made with walnuts, almonds, pistachios or even cashews. We have chosen to add pistachios to our cake; their attractive jewel-green colour adds a touch of grandeur and we find the light but strong nutty flavour works well with the sweetness. The soaking syrup can be flavoured with anything from cardamom, cloves or cinnamon to orange or lemon zest, rose or orange flower water. We have chosen to spike the syrup with rose and orange flower water, which

perfectly complement our cinnamon and nutmeg spiced sponge cake.

Sources disagree on the exact origin of baklava, different cultures lay their claim to inventing the first one – many believe that the primitive recipe came from Assyria, in approximately 8th century B.C. There are arguments from Armenia, Turkey and Istanbul to say that they created the first evolved version of baklava. Wherever it happened to originate, the recipe struck a chord with the rise of the Ottoman Empire which helped it to spread like wildfire. Soon it was the most in-demand dish, served at the tables of the rich, royal and noble. Known as 'the queen of sweets', the treats were especially popular at the tables of Sultans and their harems.

We know that the first versions of baklava were more cake-like in texture, and the Greeks lasting contribution to the recipe was the invention of ultra thin filo/phyllo pastry. The Armenians and the Arabs were said to be the first to add spices and perfumed flavourings, such as cinnamon, cloves, rose water and cardamom to the treats. As knowledge of the dessert spread, an ever-growing variety of cultures, including The Balkans, Central Asia and the Middle East developed their take on the recipe. Though many travellers must have sampled baklava on their journeys to the Middle East, it was not until the late 19th and early 20th centuries that baklava truly exported to America and Western European cuisine. We think our take on the classic recipe (see pages 104–105) manages to preserve the traditional core ingredients, while adding our own special Lola's twist.

Snake cake MOROCCO 🥄🥄🥄

This recipe is quite time-consuming, but it is worth the effort so please don't be put off! Often served at Moroccan special occasions, this cake is crisp yet unctuous and fragrant with orange flower water. The golden pastry holds a soft almond paste and the fabulous aromas truly transport you to Morocco. Delicious served with fresh mint tea.

85 g/¾ stick butter, softened

225 g/1 cup plus 2 tablespoons caster/granulated sugar

375 g/3¼ cups ground almonds

60 g/½ cup chopped shelled pistachio nuts

½ teaspoon ground cinnamon

¼ teaspoon almond extract

grated zest of 2 oranges

80 ml/scant ⅓ cup orange flower water

2 eggs

25 g/3 tablespoons plain/all-purpose flour, sifted

PASTRY

270-g/10-oz. packet of filo/phyllo pastry (you will use 5–6 sheets)

100 g/7 tablespoons butter, melted

1 egg yolk, beaten, for brushing

chopped pistachio nuts and toasted flaked/slivered almonds

MAKES 1 LARGE CAKE

Preheat the oven to 160°C (325°F) Gas 3.

Start by placing the butter and sugar into the bowl of a stand mixer fitted with the paddle attachment (or use a hand-held electric whisk and large mixing bowl) and beat on medium speed until light and fluffy. Add the ground almonds, chopped pistachios, cinnamon, almond extract, orange zest and orange flower water. Mix on medium speed until combined, then add the eggs and flour and beat until smooth.

Place a long piece of baking parchment onto your work surface. Lay a sheet of filo/phyllo pastry on top with one of the points at the top, like a diamond. Brush with melted butter. Take another sheet of pastry and position it in a diamond shape next to the first, overlapping slightly at the side. Repeat for the rest of the pastry, working across to create a long row of overlapping diamonds and brushing each sheet with melted butter as you go. Work quickly to avoid the filo/phyllo cracking and drying out in the air. You should not end up with a thick pile of sheets – they should be spread quite widely. With a knife, trim across the bottom diamond spikes to create a straight edge along the bottom.

Take the filling and carefully spoon it along the bottom of the pastry, about 5 cm/2 inches away from the edge, all along to the end of the row. This will look like a long sausage.

Carefully pick up the nearest pastry edges and roll over the almond sausage, then keep rolling until you have enclosed the almond sausage and you have a long pastry snake. To avoid the pastry cracking, you can gently scrunch the sausage so the pastry is not too tight. Take one end of the long roll and start rolling up to make a snail or coil shape. Do this carefully as you want to avoid any cracks and the filling seeping out. Lift the parchment and snake onto a baking sheet and brush with the beaten egg yolk.

Bake in the preheated oven for 30–40 minutes or until crisp and golden all over. Allow to cool before scattering over the chopped pistachios and toasted flaked/slivered almonds.

Fig and pumpkin cake TUNISIA 🥄

Inspired by trips to Tunisia and the scent of the warm spices in the air, we took some of our favourite memories, namely the dried fruits, spices and sunshine, and created this deliciously moist cake for you.

450 g/scant 3½ cups plain/all-purpose flour

1½ teaspoons baking powder

½ teaspoon bicarbonate of soda/baking soda

1 teaspoon ground cinnamon

½ teaspoon ground ginger

150 g/1¼ sticks butter, softened

300 g/1½ cups soft light brown sugar

100 g/½ cup caster/granulated sugar

½ teaspoon pure vanilla extract

4 eggs

425-g/15-oz. can puréed pumpkin

200 g/1½ cups chopped dried figs

1 tablespoon runny honey

23-cm/9-inch round loose-bottom or springform cake pan, greased and lined with baking parchment

MAKES 1 LARGE CAKE

Preheat the oven to 180°C (350°F) Gas 4.

Start by sifting the flour, baking powder, bicarbonate of soda/baking soda, cinnamon and ginger into a mixing bowl. Set aside until needed.

Place the butter, sugars and vanilla extract into the bowl of a stand mixer fitted with the paddle attachment (or use a hand-held electric whisk and large mixing bowl) and beat on medium speed for a few minutes until fluffy and fully combined.

With the motor set on slow, add the eggs, one at a time, stopping to scrape down the sides of the bowl as you go. Once all the eggs have been incorporated, carefully fold in the dry ingredients until you have a smooth batter and the mixture is a consistent colour.

Add the pumpkin and mix until just combined. Add the chopped figs, briefly mixing until evenly distributed, then pour into the prepared cake pan. Level the surface and bake in the preheated oven for 65–75 minutes or until well risen and a skewer inserted into the centre of the cake comes out clean. Allow to cool completely in the pan, but while the cake is still a little warm, drizzle the honey onto the surface of the cake to give a lovely sheen and sticky top. Once fully cooled, remove from the pan and serve.

Arab souks are fulll of jewel-bright dried fruits, sugar and spices (below).

Cairo's famous al-Fishawi cafe in Khan al-Khalili Bazaar, Egypt (below).

Tunisian mint tea (above).

Biscuits in Morocco, Africa. (above).

A man selects a piece of corn bread from a street market in Beirut, Lebanon (above).

Amarula cake

SOUTH AFRICA 🥄🥄

Amarula is a rich cream liqueur made with the marula fruit found in South Africa. Its flavour has inspired us to make this decadent cake. A dark chocolate sponge is soaked in amarula syrup and topped with a caramel cream.

60 g/¹⁄₂ cup plus 1 tablespoon unsweetened cocoa powder, sifted

125 ml/¹⁄₂ cup boiling water

3 eggs

220 g/1 cup plus 2 tablespoons caster/granulated sugar

60 ml/¹⁄₄ cup sunflower or vegetable oil

2 teaspoons baking powder

pinch of salt

250 g/1³⁄₄ cups plus 2 tablespoons plain/all-purpose flour

1 tablespoon Amarula liqueur

SYRUP

110 g/¹⁄₂ cup caster/granulated sugar

70 ml/scant ¹⁄₃ cup Amarula liqueur

TO DECORATE

200 g/¹⁄₂ cup ready-made caramel (we use the Carnation brand)

240 ml/scant 1 cup double/heavy cream

50 g/¹⁄₃ cup grated dark/bittersweet chocolate

23-cm/9-inch round loose-bottom or springform cake pan, greased and lined with baking parchment

piping/pastry bag fitted with a large plain nozzle/tip

MAKES 1 LARGE CAKE

Preheat the oven to 180°C (350°F) Gas 4.

Start by placing the cocoa into a small bowl and mixing with the boiling water. Let cool.

Place the eggs, sugar and oil into the bowl of a stand mixer fitted with the paddle attachment (or use a hand-held electric whisk and large mixing bowl) and beat on medium speed until blended. Add the cooled cocoa mixture and mix thoroughly. Add the baking powder, salt, flour and Amarula and mix well.

Pour into the prepared cake pan and bake in the preheated oven for 30–35 minutes or until well risen and a skewer inserted into the centre of the cake comes out clean. Using the skewer, prick small holes all over the cake.

Place 150 ml/²⁄₃ cup water and the sugar for the syrup into a small saucepan and bring to the boil. When the sugar has dissolved, remove the pan from the heat and add the Amarula. Slowly pour the warm syrup over the warm cake. Allow the cake to cool completely in the pan before turning out onto a serving plate.

If your cake has a pronounced dome, use a serrated knife to cut and level the top.

Take half of the caramel and smooth over the surface of the cake. Whip the cream until stiff, then add the rest of the caramel to the cream and mix again. Spoon the caramel cream into the piping/pastry bag and pipe large blobs of the cream all over the surface of the cake. Decorate with the grated chocolate and store in the fridge.

Peanut and banana cake GHANA

Paying homage to the humble peanut, this cake is truly scrumptious. The peanut grows naturally in Ghana and has pride of place in the national cake. With the addition of caramel, we think this cake is taken up a notch and could even be served warm with cream for a delicious dessert.

CAKE

225 g/2 sticks butter, softened

200 g/1 cup caster/granulated sugar

50 g/1/4 cup light soft brown sugar

3 eggs

325 g/scant 2 1/2 cups plain/all-purpose flour

2 1/2 teaspoons baking powder

pinch of salt

5 very ripe bananas, mashed with a fork

150 g/1 1/4 cups salted peanuts, chopped

CARAMEL SAUCE

150 g/3/4 cup caster/granulated sugar

150 ml/2/3 cup double/heavy cream

pinch of salt

24 x 15-cm/9 1/2 x 6-inch loaf pan, greased and lined with baking parchment

MAKES 1 LOAF CAKE

Preheat the oven to 160°C (325°F) Gas 3.

Start by making the caramel sauce. Place the sugar in a heavy-bottomed pan and heat on medium-high heat, swirling the pan until the sugar has dissolved (do not stir, as the sugar will crystallize, and keep an eye on it as it can burn very quickly). Once the caramel has melted and is turning a golden brown, turn off the heat. Very carefully, pour over the double/heavy cream, whisking as you do so. The mixture will spit and splutter, so take care. Return to the heat and bring to the boil to dissolve any sugar crystals. Add the salt, remove from the heat, then transfer to a clean bowl and set aside.

To make the cake, place the butter and sugars into the bowl of a stand mixer fitted with the paddle attachment (or use a hand-held electric whisk and large mixing bowl) and beat on medium speed until light and fluffy. Add the eggs, one at a time, making sure to scrape down the sides of the bowl after each addition.

Sift the flour, baking powder and salt into a separate bowl, and add half of this mixture to the butter mixture along with the mashed bananas. Mix to combine. Add the remaining flour mixture and two-thirds of the chopped peanuts and fold in.

Spoon half of the cake batter into the prepared pan and smooth over. Using half of the caramel sauce, place small blobs of caramel over the surface of the cake batter. This will create a delicious gooey layer of caramel through the centre of the cake. Spoon the rest of the cake batter over the caramel and level the surface, before sprinkling over the remaining chopped peanuts and placing small blobs of the remaining caramel over the top of your cake.

Bake in the centre of the preheated oven for 1 hour 20 minutes – 1 hour 30 minutes or until a skewer inserted into the centre of the cake comes out clean. Allow to cool completely in the pan before turning out and placing on a serving plate.

The Americas and the Caribbean

Banana bread USA

Red velvet cake USA

Baked vanilla and chocolate cheesecake USA

Citrus chiffon cake USA

Boston cream pie USA

Maple pecan cake CANADA

Nanaimo bars CANADA

Tres leches MEXICO

Flourless coffee cake COLOMBIA

Corn cake BRAZIL

Pastel borracho COLOMBIA

Brazil nut cake BOLIVIA

Coconut rum cake CUBA

Hummingbird cake JAMAICA

Pineapple upside-down cake JAMAICA

Ginger cake JAMAICA

Black cake TRINIDAD

Banana bread USA

There is something very comforting about a slice of banana cake. Sticky and full of flavour, yet not too sweet. This cake allows us to feel like we are being looked after by our American friend and have sat down on her porch for a tea break American-style! We urge you to wait for the cake to cool down before you eat it, but forgive you if you can't resist the temptation. This banana bread keeps really well in an airtight container and can even be toasted and served with butter.

3 large ripe bananas

1 teaspoon bicarbonate of soda/baking soda

50 ml/3½ tablespoons full-fat/whole milk

115 g/1 stick butter, softened

115 g/½ cup plus 1 tablespoon caster/granulated sugar

2 eggs

190 g self-raising flour/1½ cups minus 1 tablespoon cake flour mixed with 2½ teaspoons baking powder, sifted

24 x 15-cm/9½ x 6-inch loaf pan, greased and lined with baking parchment

MAKES 1 LOAF CAKE

Preheat the oven to 160°C (325°F) Gas 3.

Start by peeling and mashing the bananas with a fork until you have a mixture that is a combination of smooth banana and small chunks; you do not want it too smooth. Set aside until needed.

In a small bowl, mix the bicarbonate of soda/baking soda with the milk and stir until dissolved. Set aside.

Place the butter and sugar into the bowl of a stand mixer fitted with the paddle attachment (or use a hand-held electric whisk and large mixing bowl) and beat on medium speed until blended. This will take a minute or so.

Slowly add the eggs, one at a time, on low speed, stopping to scrape down the bowl occasionally. Once the eggs have been incorporated, add the mashed bananas and mix. With the speed on low, slowly add the sifted flour and the milk mixture, a little at a time, alternating between the two, until all the ingredients have been incorporated and the mixture is fully combined.

Pour the batter into the prepared loaf pan and bake in the preheated oven for 45–50 minutes or until golden brown and a skewer inserted into the centre of the cake comes out clean or with just a few crumbs attached. Leave the cake to cool completely in the pan before turning out and serving.

Red velvet cake USA

220 g/2 sticks butter, softened

320 g/1½ cups plus 1 tablespoon caster/granulated sugar

1 teaspoon pure vanilla extract

2 teaspoons red food colouring paste (natural colours won't show up)

2 eggs

70 ml/⅓ cup sunflower oil

2 tablespoons white wine vinegar or lemon juice

70 g/2½ oz. dark/bittersweet chocolate, melted

380 g/3 cups minus 2 tablespoons plain/all-purpose flour

1 teaspoon bicarbonate of soda/baking soda

2 tablespoons unsweetened cocoa powder

280 ml/1¼ cups whole milk

70 g/¾ cup ground almonds

FROSTING

120 g/1⅛ sticks butter, softened

1 teaspoon pure vanilla extract

400 g/2¾ cups icing/confectioners' sugar, sifted

800 g/1¾ lb. full-fat cream cheese

TO DECORATE

red velvet cake crumbs (we whizz any cake off-cuts into crumbs and allow them to dry out completely)

2 x 23-cm/9-inch round loose-bottom or springform cake pans, greased and lined with baking parchment

MAKES 1 LARGE CAKE

A true modern classic sent over the seas from America. The red velvet cake continues to be a best-seller at Lola's and a favourite with everyone in the Lola's team. We add melted chocolate and ground almonds to keep our vibrant cake moist and moreish, topped off with a cool cream cheese frosting… what could be better?

Preheat the oven to 180°C (350°F) Gas 4.

Place the butter, sugar and vanilla extract into the bowl of a stand mixer fitted with the paddle attachment (or use a hand-held electric whisk and large mixing bowl) and beat on medium speed until light and fluffy. This should take about 2 minutes. Add the food colouring paste and blend.

Slowly add the eggs to the mixture, one at a time, and mix until fully combined, stopping to scrape down the sides of the bowl occasionally. Add the oil and vinegar to the mixture, followed by the melted chocolate and mix until blended.

Sift all the dry ingredients into a separate bowl and slowly incorporate them into the batter, alternating with the milk, until you have a soft batter. Finally add the ground almonds and mix until smooth and a uniform colour.

Divide the batter between the prepared cake pans and bake in the preheated oven for 40–50 minutes until risen and a skewer inserted into the centre of each cake comes out clean. Turn out and allow to cool while you make the frosting.

For the frosting, put the butter into the bowl of a stand mixer fitted with the paddle attachment (or use a hand-held electric whisk and large mixing bowl) and beat until light and fluffy, then add the vanilla extract. Slowly add the icing/confectioners' sugar and the cream cheese and beat on medium-high speed until smooth and glossy. Do not over-mix.

Using a serrated knife, slice horizontally through the middle of each sponge to create four even layers. Save any crumbs for the top of the cake. If the sponges have a dome on the top, use the knife to cut this off. Place the off-cuts into a blender to create the crumbs to decorate.

Place the first sponge onto a serving plate and spread a quarter of the frosting over the cake to the edges. Top with another sponge layer and repeat. Continue in this way until you have four layers. You can either leave the cake like this or carefully spread the top icing all around the edges of the cake to create what we call a 'naked' effect – the choice is yours. Decorate with the red velvet cake crumbs.

Baked vanilla and chocolate cheesecake USA

A baked cheesecake is such an iconic American dessert. Smooth, rich and creamy, there is a multitude of flavours to try. We have updated the classic New York baked cheesecake by adding a wonderfully decadent dark chocolate swirl. We hope you enjoy it as much as we do.

BASE

160 g/6 oz. digestive biscuits/ graham crackers, crushed to crumbs

40 g/3 tablespoons butter, melted

25 g/2 tablespoons granulated sugar

FILLING

100 g/3½ oz. dark/ bittersweet chocolate (no more than 72% cocoa solids), chopped

1 kg./2 lb. full-fat cream cheese

300 g/1½ cups caster/ granulated sugar

1 teaspoon pure vanilla extract

4 eggs

TO DECORATE

unsweetened cocoa powder, to dust

23-cm/9-inch round loose-bottom or springform cake pan, greased and lined with baking parchment

MAKES 1 LARGE CHEESECAKE

Preheat the oven to 160°C (325°F) Gas 3.

Start by making the base. Mix together the digestive biscuit/ graham cracker crumbs, butter and sugar in a mixing bowl. Press into the base of the prepared cake pan and bake in the preheated oven for 10 minutes until very lightly browned. This will prevent the cheesecake base becoming soggy. Allow to cool while you make the filling.

For the filling, place the chocolate into a heatproof bowl set over a pan of gently simmering water. Do not let the bowl touch the water. Gently stir every now and then until melted. Set aside.

Place the cream cheese into the bowl of a stand mixer fitted with the paddle attachment (or use a hand-held electric whisk and large mixing bowl) and beat on medium speed until smooth and light. Add the sugar and vanilla extract and beat to incorporate. Once combined, add the eggs, one at a time, stopping to scrape down the sides of the bowl as you go to make sure all the ingredients are incorporated. Pour two-thirds of the mixture over the cooled base.

Carefully pour the melted chocolate into the remaining cream cheese mixture and beat to combine. This mixture will be stiffer than the vanilla mix as the chocolate will set slightly. Take spoonfuls of the chocolate mixture and dollop it into the vanilla mixture in random places until you have used it all. Use the handle of a spoon to run the chocolate into the vanilla, creating a swirl effect, gently blending the two flavours together.

Bake in the preheated oven for 50–60 minutes or until the cheesecake is almost set; the edges will puff up slightly but there should still be a slight wobble in the centre of the cheesecake when gently shaken. Turn off the oven and leave the cheesecake to cool in the oven. Remove from the oven once cooled and place straight into the fridge to chill for at least 2 hours. Run a palette knife or metal spatula around the edges of the pan and remove the cheesecake. Place it onto a serving plate and dust generously with cocoa powder to serve.

Citrus chiffon cake USA DF 🥄🥄🥄

If you have never tried a chiffon cake, we urge you to give this recipe a go. Invented in the USA in the 1920s, this incredibly light and flavoursome cake is bound to be a crowd-pleaser.

175 g/1⅓ cups plain/all-purpose flour, sifted

1½ teaspoons baking powder

½ teaspoon salt

225 g/1 cup plus 2 tablespoons caster/granulated sugar

3 egg yolks

8 egg whites

5 tablespoons vegetable oil

1 teaspoon pure vanilla extract

grated zest of 3 oranges and freshly squeezed juice of 1 large orange (approx.150 ml/⅔ cup)

grated zest of 1 large lemon

¾ teaspoon cream of tartar

ICING

freshly squeezed juice of 1 lemon

250 g/1¾ cups icing/confectioners' sugar

grated or pared orange or lemon zest

25-cm/10-inch angel food cake pan or tube pan

MAKES 1 LARGE CAKE

Preheat the oven to 180°C (350°F) Gas 4.

Into a large bowl, sift the flour, baking powder and salt. Stir in 200 g/ 1 cup of the caster/granulated sugar. Set aside the remaining sugar for later.

In another bowl, combine the 3 egg yolks (set aside the 8 egg whites for later) oil, vanilla, orange and lemon zests and orange juice. Using a whisk, add this to the bowl containing the flour and sugar and blend until smooth.

Place the 8 egg whites into the bowl of a stand mixer fitted with a whisk attachment (or use a hand-held electric whisk and large mixing bowl) and whisk on high speed until foamy. Add the cream of tartar and beat until soft peaks form. Gradually add the remaining sugar on high speed until stiff peaks form and the mixture is glossy. Using a spatula, fold a quarter of this mixture into the orange mixture. Gently fold in the remaining whites until fully combined.

Spoon the batter into the ungreased angel food pan and smooth the surface. Bake in the preheated oven for 50–55 minutes until the cake springs back to the touch. Remove from the oven and cool in the pan for 10 minutes before inverting the pan and allowing the cake to cool completely upside down in the pan.

To make the icing, slowly add the lemon juice to the sifted icing/confectioners' sugar until you have a runny consistency. Once the cake is fully cool, remove from the pan and drizzle the icing over the inverted cake. Decorate with orange or lemon zest to serve.

Boston cream pie USA 🥄🥄🥄

Boston cream pie is now the official cake of Massachusetts, but its history dates back to the 1850s when it was created by the Parker House Hotel. The crème légère filling needs to chill for a minimum of three hours, or ideally overnight.

CRÈME LÉGÈRE FILLING

350 ml/scant 1½ cups full-fat/whole milk

80 g/scant ½ cup caster/granulated sugar

1 teaspoon vanilla bean paste

4 egg yolks

40 g/generous ¼ cup plain/all-purpose flour

1 tablespoon corn flour/cornstarch

200 ml/⅔ cup double/heavy cream

GENOISE SPONGE

9 eggs

300 g/1½ cups caster/granulated sugar

240 g/1¾ cups plain/all-purpose flour, sifted

35 g/¼ cup cornflour/cornstarch, sifted

45 g/3½ tablespoons butter, melted and cooled

TOPPING

100 ml/½ cup double/heavy cream

75 g/⅓ cup plus 2 teaspoons light soft brown sugar

100 g/3½ oz. dark/bittersweet chocolate, chopped

4 teaspoons vegetable oil

23-cm/9-inch round loose-bottom or springform cake pan, greased and lined with baking parchment

MAKES 1 LARGE CAKE

First, make the crème légère filling. Place the milk, 30 g/2½ tablespoons of the sugar and the vanilla in a saucepan and heat until almost boiling. In another large bowl beat together the egg yolks and remaining sugar until combined, then add the flours and whisk together.

Slowly pour the hot milk over the egg mixture, beating continuously. Pour back into the pan and heat over medium heat, whisking continuously for about 5 minutes until thickened and simmering. Pour into a large bowl and cover with clingfilm/plastic wrap to avoid a skin forming. Refrigerate for at least 3 hours or ideally overnight. Preheat the oven to 160°C (325°F) Gas 3.

For the sponge, place the eggs into the bowl of a stand mixer fitted with the whisk attachment (or use a hand-held electric whisk and large mixing bowl) and beat on medium speed until white and foamy. Increase the speed and slowly add the sugar, mixing until the mixture has doubled in size.

In a separate bowl, sift together the flour and cornflour/cornstarch and fold carefully into the egg mixture using a metal spoon. Lastly, fold in the cooled, melted butter. Pour the batter into the prepared pan and bake in the preheated oven for 50–60 minutes or until golden and well risen.

Cool in the pan for 10 minutes before turning out and placing in the fridge to firm up.

Once cooled, beat the filling with a whisk until smooth. In another bowl, whip the double/heavy cream to soft peaks. Slowly whisk the cream into the custard until smooth and light. Set aside.

For the topping, place the cream and brown sugar into a small saucepan with 100 ml/⅓ cup water and simmer for a few minutes until the sugar has dissolved. Place the chocolate in a heatproof bowl and pour the hot liquid over. Stir until melted and smooth. Leave to cool for 30 minutes before stirring in the vegetable oil. Set aside.

To assemble the cake, use a serrated knife to cut the cake into two even halves. Spread the crème légère filling over the bottom half of sponge before carefully sandwiching the other half on top. Pour the chocolate topping over the surface of the cake and allow to drip down over the sides. Allow to set before serving.

Maple pecan cake CANADA

The wonderful smoky aroma of maple syrup and the crisp texture of pecans team up beautifully in this fabulous Bundt cake. With a maple glaze and mellow vanilla sponge, this cake is proud to be of Canadian origin!

260 g/2 cups plain/all-purpose flour, sifted

110 g/½ cup plus 1 tablespoon caster/granulated sugar

120 g/½ cup soft light brown sugar

1 teaspoon bicarbonate of soda/baking soda

pinch of salt

180 ml/¾ cup full-fat/whole milk

100 g/½ cup natural/plain yogurt

100 g/7 tablespoons butter, melted

100 ml/⅓ cup pure dark maple syrup

1 teaspoon pure vanilla extract

80 g/⅔ cup chopped pecan nuts

GLAZE

200 g/1½ cups icing/confectioners' sugar

pinch of ground cinnamon

50 ml/¼ cup dark maple syrup, or more if needed

DECORATION

25 g/¼ cup chopped pecan nuts

26-cm/10½-inch Bundt or decorative ring mould pan, greased and floured

MAKES 1 LARGE CAKE

Preheat the oven to 180°C (350°F) Gas 4.

Place the flour, sugars, bicarbonate of soda/baking soda and salt into a large bowl. In another bowl, mix together the milk, yogurt, melted butter, maple syrup and vanilla extract. Carefully stir the wet ingredients into the dry ingredients and blend until just combined. Add the chopped pecans and mix.

Spoon the mixture into the prepared Bundt pan or ring mould and bake in the preheated oven for 30–40 minutes or until well risen and a skewer inserted into the centre of the cake comes out clean. Allow to cool in the pan for 10 minutes before turning out onto a serving plate and allowing to cool completely.

To make the glaze, sift the icing/confectioners' sugar and cinnamon into a large bowl and slowly incorporate the maple syrup using a wooden spoon. Beat the glaze until smooth. Drizzle over the cooled cake, allowing the glaze to trickle down the sides and centre. Sprinkle with the chopped pecans and enjoy.

Nanaimo bars

CANADA

The creator of this creamy, chocolatey treat remains unknown. We do know that the bar originates from Nanaimo, a city on Vancouver Island. We think they are delicious and a great recipe to make with small children as they require no baking whatsoever. The recipe is divided into three parts – a digestive biscuit/graham cracker and coconut base, vanilla custard middle and top layer of chocolate ganache. Together they make the most delicious chocolate bar for any occasion. Thank you, Canada!

BOTTOM LAYER

115 g/1 stick butter

50 g/¼ cup white sugar

80 g/¾ cup unsweetened cocoa powder

1 egg, beaten

200 g/7 oz. digestive biscuits/graham crackers, crushed to crumbs

50 g/½ cup finely chopped almonds

100 g/1⅓ cups desiccated/dried unsweetened shredded coconut

MIDDLE LAYER

115 g/1 stick butter

50 ml/¼ cup double/heavy cream

30 g/¼ cup custard powder/instant vanilla pudding mix

250 g/1¾ cups icing/confectioners' sugar,

TOP LAYER

100 g/3½ oz. dark/bittersweet chocolate (no more than 70% cocoa solids), chopped

50 g/2 oz. milk chocolate, chopped

50 g/3½ tablespoons butter

20-cm/8-inch square brownie pan, greased and lined with baking parchment

MAKES 8 BARS

For the bottom layer, place the butter, sugar and cocoa powder into a small pan and melt over a gentle heat until the sugar has dissolved. Remove from the heat, add the egg and stir briskly to incorporate. The residual heat from the mixture will cook the egg and thicken the mixture. Stir in the digestive biscuit/graham cracker crumbs, chopped almonds and coconut. Press firmly into the prepared brownie pan using your fingertips.

For the middle layer, put the butter, cream, custard powder/instant vanilla pudding mix, and icing/confectioners' sugar into the bowl of a stand mixer fitted with the paddle attachment (or use a hand-held electric whisk and large mixing bowl) and beat on low speed until light and fully blended. Spread evenly over the bottom chocolate layer.

For the top layer, place both types of chocolate and the butter into a small pan and melt together over low heat. Remove from the heat and allow to cool for 5 minutes until a little cooler but still liquid. Pour over the middle layer and chill in the refrigerator for at least 4 hours or until set. Remove from the pan and carefully cut into 8 bars.

Tres leches MEXICO

Tres leches means 'three milks' and this delicious cake contains a mixture of double/heavy cream, condensed milk and evaporated milk. It is not for the faint-hearted! A southern American favourite inspired by Nestlé and their factories throughout southern America, in our opinion this is one not to be missed.

6 eggs, separated

450 g/2¼ cups caster/granulated sugar

1 teaspoon pure vanilla extract

230 g/1¾ cups plain/all-purpose flour

2 teaspoons baking powder

125 ml/½ cup full-fat/whole milk

THREE MILKS

300 ml/1¼ cups double/heavy cream

410-g/14-oz. can evaporated milk

400-g/14-oz. can condensed milk

FILLING

400-g/14-oz. can ready-made caramel

300 ml/1¼ cups double/heavy cream, softly whipped

TO FINISH

500 ml/2 cups double/heavy cream

1 tablespoon icing/confectioners' sugar, sifted

1 teaspoon pure vanilla extract

30 g/⅓ cup toasted flaked/slivered almonds

23-cm/9-inch round loose-bottom or springform cake pan, greased and lined with baking parchment

MAKES 1 LARGE CAKE

Preheat the oven to 160°C (325°F) Gas 3.

Place the egg whites and half of the sugar into the bowl of a stand mixer fitted with the whisk attachment (or use a hand-held electric whisk and large mixing bowl) and beat on medium speed until soft peaks form. Add the remaining sugar and beat until stiff peaks form.

Add the egg yolks, one at a time, and the vanilla extract while mixing on slow speed. Gently fold in the flour and baking powder, alternating with the milk.

Transfer to the prepared cake pan and bake in the preheated oven for 50–60 minutes until well risen, golden and a skewer inserted into the centre of the cake comes out clean. Allow to cool in the pan completely while you make the three milks.

Place all three 'milks' into a pan and heat on medium heat until melted together and just coming up to the boil. Stir to stop the mixture catching on the bottom of the pan. Set aside to cool.

Remove the cooled sponge from the pan. Using a serrated knife, slice horizontally through the sponge to create three even layers.

Place the first layer onto a serving plate and soak with the cooled three milks mixture. We do this by spooning over a generous amount of the milks. It should feel soggy to the touch.

Spread half of the caramel over this layer and then half of the whipped cream. Repeat the layers, finishing with a layer of sponge. Soak this layer, but don't worry if you have some of the three milks left over. Cover the cake and chill for at least 4 hours or overnight.

To finish, place the cream, icing/confectioners' sugar and vanilla extract in the bowl of a stand mixer fitted with the whisk attachment (or use a hand-held electric whisk and large mixing bowl) and beat until you have softly whipped cream.

Spread a thick layer of the whipped cream onto the top of the cake and carefully, using a palette knife or metal spatula, spread it so that it starts to cascade over the sides. Cover the cake roughly with all the remaining whipped cream mixture – we think the it looks beautiful with soft ruffles. Carefully press the flaked/slivered almonds into the cream around the bottom of the cake. It doesn't need to be perfect. Sit back and admire your creation before tucking in!

Emergency cake on its way in New York City, (right).

Georgetown Cafe & Bakery in Virginia, USA (above).

The famous Cake Boss Cafe in Midtown Manhattan, USA (right).

What a selection! Treats on display at the Cheesecake Factory Inc. Kentucky, USA (left).

A perfect porch on which to eat cake in Upstate New York, USA (right).

A store dedicated to the Southern delicacy of Key Lime Pie in Florida, USA (left).

Flourless coffee cake

COLOMBIA GF

This is a brilliantly indulgent gluten-free recipe inspired by two of our favourite ingredients – coffee and chocolate. South America really knows how to create some of the best in the world, so we thought why not combine the two ingredients to create this decadent cake. To up the coffee intensity, serve with a rich shot of espresso and enjoy.

300 g/10½ oz. dark/bittersweet chocolate (we like to use a combination of 50% and 70% cocoa solids), chopped

275 g/2½ sticks butter

30 ml/⅛ cup strong fresh espresso

2 teaspoons instant espresso powder

6 eggs, separated

100 g/½ cup caster/granulated sugar

300 g/3 cups ground almonds

unsweetened cocoa powder or icing/confectioners' sugar, to decorate

23-cm/9-inch round loose-bottom or springform cake pan, greased and lined with baking parchment

MAKES 1 LARGE CAKE

Preheat the oven to 160°C (325°F) Gas 3.

Place the chocolate, butter, espresso and espresso powder into a heatproof bowl set over a pan of simmering water and gently melt, stirring occasionally. Make sure the bottom of the bowl doesn't touch the water. Once melted, set aside until needed.

Meanwhile, place the egg yolks and sugar in a bowl and, either by hand or with a hand-held electric whisk, beat together until thick and pale, about 3 minutes with a hand-held electric whisk.

Fold the chocolate mixture into the egg and sugar mixture using a metal spoon or rubber, then fold in the ground almonds.

In a separate clean bowl, whisk the egg whites to stiff peaks. Fold the egg whites into the cake mixture and transfer to the prepared cake pan. Bake in the preheated oven for 35–40 minutes or until risen and a skewer inserted into the centre of the cake comes out almost clean. (You can under-bake this cake by 5 minutes to create more of a pudding texture if you prefer.)

Allow to cool completely in the pan before removing and carefully placing on a serving plate. Dust lightly with cocoa powder or icing/confectioners' sugar before serving.

Corn cake BRAZIL

Known as *bolo de fubá* in Brazil, this corn cake is found in many Brazilian homes and is traditionally served for breakfast with a piping hot cup of coffee. You will find many variations of this cake with different additions. Here, we have made the cake moist and sticky by adding a tangy lime syrup soak.

CAKE

125 g/³⁄₄ cup polenta or fine cornmeal

125 g/1 cup minus 1 tablespoon plain/all-purpose flour

2¹⁄₂ teaspoons baking powder

pinch of salt

225 g/1 cup plus 2 tablespoons caster/granulated sugar

2 eggs

120 ml/¹⁄₂ cup double/heavy cream

120 ml/¹⁄₂ cup warm water

120ml/¹⁄₂ cup vegetable oil

¹⁄₂ teaspoon pure vanilla extract

SYRUP SOAK

freshly squeezed juice of 2 large limes

grated zest of 1 lime

80 g/²⁄₃ cup icing/confectioners' sugar, sifted

26-cm/10¹⁄₂-inch Bundt or decorative ring mould pan, greased and floured

MAKES 1 LARGE CAKE

Preheat the oven to 160°C (325°F) Gas 3.

To make the cake, place all the dry cake ingredients (the polenta or cornmeal, flour, baking powder, salt and sugar) into the bowl of a stand mixer fitted with the paddle attachment (or use a hand-held electric whisk and large mixing bowl).

In a separate mixing bowl, beat together the wet cake ingredients (eggs, cream, water, oil and vanilla extract). With the mixer on low, slowly incorporate the wet ingredients into the dry and mix until well combined and smooth. Do not over-mix.

Spoon the mixture into the prepared Bundt pan or ring mould and spread out with a spatula. Bake in the preheated oven for 45–50 minutes or until a skewer inserted into the centre of the cake comes out clean. Allow to cool in the pan for 20 minutes before carefully turning out onto a wire rack to cool completely. Using a cocktail stick/toothpick, prick the cake all over in preparation for the syrup soak.

To make the syrup, place all the syrup ingredients into a small saucepan and heat gently, stirring, until the sugar has dissolved. Remove from the heat and allow to cool for 5 minutes before carefully spooning over the cooled corn cake and allowing it to soak into the small holes. Allow the cake to sit for an hour or so to allow all the flavours to mingle, before slicing and serving.

Pastel borracho COLOMBIA

This Colombian delicacy has a dense and buttery Madeira-type sponge, which is soaked in both rum syrup and crème Anglaise. Another favourite with Julia our baker, she likes to serve this at the end of a barbecue to send guests home happy!

420 g/scant 3¼ cups plain/all-purpose flour

½ teaspoon baking powder

½ teaspoon bicarbonate of soda/baking soda

pinch of salt

225 g/2 sticks butter

400 g/2 cups caster/granulated sugar

4 eggs

180 ml/¾ cup full-fat/whole milk

1½ teaspoon pure vanilla extract

RUM SYRUP

100 g/½ cup caster/granulated sugar

80 ml/scant ⅓ cup dark rum

150 g/1 cup dried pitted prunes/dried plums

CRÈME ANGLAISE

120 ml/½ cup evaporated milk

120 ml/½ cup double/heavy cream

1 teaspoon pure vanilla extract

4 egg yolks

20 g/1 tablespoon plus 2 teaspoons caster/granulated sugar

26-cm/10½-inch Bundt or decorative ring mould pan, greased and floured

MAKES 1 LARGE CAKE

Preheat the oven to 180°C (350°F) Gas 4.

Start by making the cake. Combine the flour, baking powder, bicarbonate of soda/baking soda and salt in a bowl.

Place the butter and sugar into the bowl of a stand mixer fitted with the paddle attachment (or use a hand-held electric whisk and large mixing bowl) and beat on medium speed until light and fluffy. Beat in the eggs, one at a time, alternating with the milk and stopping to scrape down the sides of the bowl. Mix in the vanilla extract.

Turn the motor off and carefully add the combined dry ingredients. Mix on medium speed until combined. Do not over-mix.

Pour the batter into the prepared Bundt pan or ring mould and bake in the preheated oven for 50–60 minutes until golden brown and risen and a skewer inserted into the centre comes out clean. Allow to cool in the pan for 30 minutes before turning out onto a wire rack.

Use a serrated knife to slice the cooled cake in half. Set aside.

To make the rum syrup, place the sugar and 120 ml/½ cup water into a small heavy saucepan and heat on medium heat until the sugar has dissolved. Boil for a few minutes to reduce the liquid. Remove from the heat and add the rum and prunes/dried plums. Set aside to cool.

For the crème Anglaise, place the evaporated milk, cream, vanilla, egg yolks and sugar into a bowl and beat using a balloon whisk until well combined. Pour the mixture into a heavy-bottomed saucepan and bring to a simmer over low heat. Stir the custard constantly for 7–8 minutes with a whisk or wooden spoon until thickened. Do not let the custard boil. Remove from the heat and allow to cool.

To assemble the cake, place the bottom sponge layer onto a cake stand or plate and brush the top liberally with the cooled rum syrup, letting it soak in. Drizzle over one-third of the crème Anglaise and allow it to soak in (it is ok if it dribbles down the sides).

Remove the prunes/dried plums from the syrup and place them in a layer on top of the sponge, reserving two for decoration. Sandwich the top layer of sponge on and brush liberally all over with the rum syrup. Brush or drizzle the remaining crème Anglaise over the cake. Slice the reserved prunes/dried plums into small slithers and use to decorate the finished cake. Allow to sit in the fridge for at least an hour before eating to allow most of the syrup to be absorbed. Enjoy!

Brazil nut cake

BOLIVIA 🥄

Brazil nut cake, or *bolo de castan has
do pará*, is a popular treat in Bolivia,
as well as other Amazon regions,
thanks to the prevalence of the brazil
nut tree in the region. Originally
served as a dessert, we have turned
it into a gorgeous teatime cake.
Ground Brazil nuts in the sponge
add a richness and wonderful
texture, and fragrant rum and
coconut make this a real treat.

225 g/2 sticks butter, softened

225 g/1 cup plus 2 tablespoons
caster/granulated sugar

3 eggs

190 g/1½ cups minus 1
tablespoon plain/all-purpose flour

pinch of salt

100 g/¾ cup Brazil nuts, ground

1 teaspoon pure vanilla extract

1 teaspoon baking powder

1½ tablespoons dark rum

60 g/¾ cup desiccated/dried
unsweetened shredded coconut

235 ml/scant 1 cup full-fat/ whole
milk

30 g/1 oz. Brazil nuts, sliced

23-cm/9-inch round loose-bottom
or springform cake pan, greased
and lined with baking parchment

MAKES 1 LARGE CAKE

Preheat the oven to 180°C (350°F) Gas 4.

Place the butter and sugar into the bowl of a stand mixer fitted
with a paddle attachment (or use a hand-held electric whisk and
large mixing bowl). Mix on low speed until soft, fluffy and fully
blended. Next, add the eggs, one at a time, with the mixer running
slowly, until fully combined. Finally, add the flour, salt, the ground
Brazil nuts, vanilla extract, baking powder, rum, coconut and milk.
Mix until fully combined.

Pour the mixture into the prepared cake pan. Adorn the surface
of the cake with the sliced Brazil nuts in a pretty pattern around the
outside edge and finishing with a star-shape in the middle. Bake in
the preheated oven for 45–55 minutes until the top is golden and
springs back when gently touched with your fingertip. Allow to
cool in the pan for about 15 minutes, then turn out onto a serving
plate to cool completely before serving.

Coconut rum cake CUBA

Anything flavoured with coconut and rum makes us dream of warmer climates. This tropical tasting cake will transport you to your own sun-drenched paradise.

375 g/3¾ sticks butter

275 g/1½ cups minus 2 tablespoons caster/granulated sugar

4 eggs, plus 3 egg yolks

200 g/1½ cups plain/all-purpose flour

45 g/½ cup desiccated/dried unsweetened shredded coconut

1½ teaspoons baking powder

2 tablespoons dark rum

FROSTING

75 g/¾ stick butter, softened

150 g/1 cup icing/confectioners' sugar, sifted

½ teaspoon pure vanilla extract

1½ tablespoons dark rum

TO DECORATE

desiccated/dried unsweetened shredded coconut

23-cm/9-inch round loose-bottom or springform cake pan, greased and lined with baking parchment

MAKES 1 LARGE CAKE

Preheat the oven to 180°C (350°F) Gas 4.

Melt the butter and set aside. Place the sugar, eggs and egg yolks into the bowl of a stand mixer fitted with the whisk attachment (or use a hand-held electric whisk and large mixing bowl) and whisk until light, fluffy and pale in colour.

Fold in the flour, coconut and baking powder. Slowly stir in the melted butter until combined.

Spoon the batter into the prepared cake pan and smooth the surface. Bake in the preheated oven for 40–50 minutes until the cake springs back to the touch. Cool in the pan for 10 minutes, then turn out onto a wire rack and sprinkle the rum over the cake. Allow to cool completely.

To make the frosting, place the butter into the bowl of a stand mixer fitted with the paddle attachment (or use a hand-held electric whisk and large mixing bowl) and carefully add the icing/confectioners' sugar with the mixer on slow speed. Once combined, increase the speed and add the vanilla extract and rum, mixing to make a soft buttercream frosting.

Spread a thin layer of frosting over the sides of the cake with a palette knife or metal spatula. Add a thicker layer to the top of the cake and drag the palette knife gently from the centre of the frosting outwards in curved lines all the way around to create a softly ruffled finish. Finally, press the coconut into the sides and onto the top edge of the cake to decorate.

Hummingbird cake JAMAICA

At Lola's we love the hummingbird cake, which was created on the island of Jamaica and named after their national bird. Layers of lightly spiced and moist sponge cake spiked with banana, pineapple and coconut are encased in a delicious cream cheese frosting. Similar to carrot cake in texture, this cake would be a welcome addition to any tea party.

280 g/2 cups plus 2 tablespoons plain/all-purpose flour, sifted

120 g/²⁄₃ cup soft light brown sugar

120 g/²⁄₃ cup caster/granulated sugar

¾ teaspoon baking powder *soda*

½ teaspoon ground cinnamon

pinch of salt

2 eggs

115 ml/⅓ cup plus 1 tablespoon vegetable oil

1 teaspoon pure vanilla extract

170 g/²⁄₃ cup canned crushed pineapple, drained, or finely chopped fresh pineapple

2 bananas, roughly mashed

75 g/1 cup desiccated/dried unsweetened shredded coconut

75 g/²⁄₃ cup chopped pecans or nuts of your choice

FROSTING

450 g/1 lb. full-fat cream cheese

75 g/¾ stick butter, softened

200 g/1½ cups icing/confectioners' sugar

1 teaspoon pure vanilla extract

1 teaspoon grated orange zest

100 g/1 cup chopped pecans or nuts of your choice, plus a few pecan halves to decorate

2 x 23-cm/9-inch round loose-bottom or springform cake pans, greased and lined with baking parchment

MAKES 1 LARGE CAKE

Preheat the oven to 180°C (350°F) Gas 4.

Combine the flour, sugars, baking powder, cinnamon and salt in a large mixing bowl. Stir in the eggs, oil and vanilla extract until the mixture looks a little sandy. Carefully stir through the pineapple, bananas and coconut until the batter is blended. Do not beat the mixture as this will create a tough batter. Stir through the chopped pecans and divide the mixture evenly between the prepared cake pans. Level the surface and bake in the preheated oven for 25–35 minutes or until risen and golden brown. Allow to cool completely in the pans before turning out.

To make the frosting, place the cream cheese and butter into the bowl of a stand mixer fitted with a paddle attachment (or use a hand-held electric whisk and large mixing bowl) and beat to combine. Carefully add the icing/confectioners' sugar and slowly beat together, being sure to do this on slow speed so as not to coat your kitchen in a cloud of icing/confectioners' sugar! Once combined, increase the speed, add the vanilla extract and orange zest, and beat until you have a soft and fluffy mixture.

Using a serrated knife, slice each cake in half horizontally through the middle to create four even sponge layers in total.

Place one layer onto a serving plate. Spread just under a quarter of the cream cheese frosting onto this layer, and then repeat with each layer until you have a four-layer cake that is topped with frosting. Smooth the remaining frosting over the sides of the cake with a palette knife or metal spatula to give a rustic 'naked' effect. Sprinkle the chopped pecans around the top edge and decorate the centre with pecan nut halves. Refrigerate the cake for at least 1 hour before serving to allow the cream cheese frosting to set.

Pineapple upside-down cake JAMAICA

This is a retro classic that we have updated with a gently spiced ginger element. Both pineapple and ginger are commonly found in recipes from Jamaica, so what better way to marry them together than in this lovely bake? This wonderful cake is delicious served cold or warm for dessert and really shows off the sweet and juicy nature of pineapple. We used canned pineapple in this recipe as it releases more juices, however, feel free to experiment with fresh.

TOPPING

75 g/¾ stick butter

60 g/⅓ cup minus 1 tablespoon light soft brown sugar

1 tablespoon golden/light corn syrup

430-g/15-oz. can pineapple rings in natural juice, drained and patted dry

75 g/3 oz. candied ginger, chopped

CAKE

120 g/4 oz. marzipan/almond paste

280 g/2½ sticks butter, softened

280 g/1½ cups caster/granulated sugar

4 eggs

280 g self-raising flour/2¼ cups cake flour mixed with 4 teaspoons baking powder, sifted

1 teaspoon pure vanilla extract

50 g/2 oz. candied ginger, chopped

GLAZE

1 tablespoon golden/light corn syrup

23-cm/9-inch round loose-bottom or springform cake pan, greased and base-lined with baking parchment

MAKES 1 LARGE CAKE

Preheat the oven to 160°C (325°F) Gas 3.

Take the butter for the topping and squash it evenly into the base of the prepared cake pan. Sprinkle all over with the brown sugar, making sure to cover all the butter and use it all. Drizzle the golden/light corn syrup over the brown sugar and then arrange the pineapple rings on top – start in the middle and work outwards. Take the candied ginger and fill in the hole of each pineapple ring with ginger pieces.

To make the cake, place the marzipan/almond paste, butter and sugar into the bowl of a stand mixer fitted with the paddle attachment (or use a hand-held electric whisk and large mixing bowl) and beat on medium speed until light and fluffy. Add the eggs, one at a time, stopping to scrape down the sides of the bowl as you go.

Add the flour and vanilla extract to the eggs and gently fold in until just combined. Spoon half of the cake mixture over the pineapple rings in the pan.

Scatter over the candied ginger and then spoon the remaining cake mixture over the ginger, spreading it evenly.

Level the surface and place the cake pan on a baking sheet to catch any leaking butter and sugar. Bake in the preheated oven for 60–70 minutes until well risen and golden brown. Allow to cool in the pan for 20 minutes.

Loosen the edges using a knife and then invert the cake onto a serving plate – be careful as there may be some hot juices released from the pineapple. Drizzle the golden/light corn syrup over to glaze. Leave to cool a little or completely to room temperature before serving.

Confeitaria Colombo, a grand old cafe in Rio de Janeiro, Brazil (above).

A Brazilian bolo de fubá or corn cake served in the sunshine. Try our recipe on page 140 (right).

Coffee and cake are the perfect pairing in any language... a hand-painted sign in Panajachel, Guatemala (left).

A careful cake delivery via bicycle in Santiago de Cuba, Cuba (right).

Fancy cake decorating in the aptly named city of Sucre, Bolivia (left).

Ginger cake JAMAICA

Our ginger cake isn't the typical dark and dense loaf, but a light fragrant sponge studded with spicy stem ginger. The glorious warmth is complemented by cool cream cheese frosting.

Preheat the oven to 180°C (350°F) Gas 4.

Place the butter, sugars and black treacle/molasses into the bowl of a stand mixer fitted with the paddle attachment (or use a hand-held electric whisk and large mixing bowl) and beat on medium speed until light and fluffy, about 2 minutes.

Slowly add the eggs, one at a time, making sure you scrape down the sides of the bowl after each addition.

Into another bowl, sift together the flour, baking powder and ground ginger. With the speed set on low, slowly add the flour mixture to the creamed butter mixture, mixing until fully combined. Turn off the motor and fold in the chopped stem ginger and sour cream.

Pour the mixture evenly into the prepared pan. Bake in the preheated oven for 45–50 minutes or until well risen and a skewer inserted into the centre of the cake comes out clean. Allow to cool completely in the pan.

While the cake is cooling make the cream cheese frosting. Beat the butter in a stand mixer fitted with a paddle attachment (or use a hand-held electric whisk and large mixing bowl) until light and fluffy. Add the cream cheese and double/heavy cream and blend. Carefully, with the speed on low, add the icing/confectioners' sugar, then beat on medium- high speed until smooth and glossy. This will take about 20 seconds – do not over-mix.

To assemble the cake, carefully remove the cake from the pan and place on a serving plate. Spoon the frosting over the top of the cake and allow it to run over the sides a little (you may need to use the spoon to encourage this). Finally, scatter with some extra chopped stem ginger to decorate, and serve.

185 g/1½ sticks butter, softened

150 g/¾ cup caster/granulated sugar

150 g/¾ cup soft light brown sugar

1 tablespoon black treacle/molasses

5 eggs

210 g self-raising flour/1½ cups cake flour mixed with 3 teaspoons baking powder, sifted

1 teaspoon baking powder

2½ teaspoons ground ginger

75 g/3 oz. preserved stem ginger, chopped, plus extra to decorate

185 ml/¾ cup sour cream

FROSTING

20 g/1½ tablespoons butter, softened

180 g/¾ cup full-fat cream cheese

40 ml/scant ¼ cup double/heavy cream

60 g/½ cup icing/confectioners' sugar, sifted

26-cm/10½-inch Bundt or decorative ring mould pan, greased and floured

MAKES 1 LARGE CAKE

Black cake TRINIDAD

This is a delicious dense fruit cake best suited to a special occasion such as Christmas or Thanksgiving. It combines wonderful juicy dried fruits with warm spices and dark rum to create a really special and quite boozy cake. The title suggests the cake is black, however, our cake is a little lighter in appearance than its forefathers. It's best to start a few days before you want to eat the cake to allow the fruits to soak up lots of flavour.

125 g/⅔ cup (dark) raisins

100 g/¾ cup currants

100 g/¾ cup dried pitted prunes, chopped

25 g/¼ cup mixed/candied peel

100 ml/⅓ cup kirsch

250 ml/1 cup dark rum

225 g/2 sticks butter, softened

225 g/1 cup plus 2 tablespoons soft dark brown sugar

5 eggs, beaten

1 teaspoon pure vanilla extract

225 g/1¾ cups plain/all-purpose flour, sifted

1½ teaspoons ground cinnamon

½ teaspoon ground ginger

½ teaspoon ground nutmeg

¼ teaspoon ground cloves

2 teaspoons baking powder

23-cm/9-inch round loose-bottom or springform cake pan, greased and lined with baking parchment (be sure to line the base and sides to protect the mixture as it cooks)

MAKES 1 LARGE CAKE

Start your cake by soaking the fruits. The amount of time you soak them for is entirely up to you: it must be no less than 6 hours, but they can be kept in an airtight sterilized glass jar for up to 6 months to soak. We like to place our fruits (the (dark) raisins, currants, prunes and mixed/candied peel) into a glass bowl with the kirsch and rum, cover and set aside to work its magic. We urge you to try and give the fruits at least an overnight soak if possible.

Preheat the oven to 160°C (325°F) Gas 3.

When you are ready to bake the cake, take half of the soaked fruits and purée them with any remaining soaking liquid to a coarse dark paste in a food processor. Keep the remaining soaked fruits whole and add the coarse purée back to the bowl.

Place the butter and sugar into the bowl of a stand mixer fitted with the paddle attachment (or use a hand-held electric whisk and large mixing bowl) and beat on medium speed until pale and fluffy.

Slowly pour the beaten eggs and vanilla into the mixture, stopping to scrape down the sides of the bowl as you go. Once fully combined, add the flour, spices and baking powder and combine on slow speed until fully blended. Using a wooden spoon or spatula, add the mixture of soaked and blended fruits into the batter and mix through.

Spoon into the prepared cake pan and place in the centre of the preheated oven for 80–90 minutes (checking after 80 minutes) or until risen and a skewer inserted into the centre of the cake comes out clean. If the cake becomes too dark on the surface partway through baking, you can cover it with some foil to prevent darkening any further. Allow to cool completely in the pan.

We find this cake is best kept for a few days before eating so that all the flavours can meld together. If you are going to store the cake, wrap it in baking parchment and then foil to ensure the cake is fully sealed. It will keep for a number of weeks stored this way.

Australasia and Asia

Chocolate mud cake AUSTRALIA

Lamingtons AUSTRALIA

Carrot cake AUSTRALIA

Lolly cake NEW ZEALAND

Pavlova NEW ZEALAND

Toffee macadamia cake NEW ZEALAND

Coconut cake FIJI

Matcha cake JAPAN

Castella cake JAPAN

Sesame cake INDIA

Mango cake BURMA

Honey cake RUSSIA

Chocolate mud cake AUSTRALIA

400 g/3½ sticks butter, chopped

200 g/7 oz. good-quality dark/bittersweet chocolate, chopped (no more than 70% cocoa solids)

60 g/⅔ cup unsweetened cocoa powder, sifted

3 tablespoons instant espresso powder

1½ teaspoons pure vanilla extract

440 g/2 cups caster/ granulated sugar

6 eggs

230 g self-raising flour/ 1¾ cups cake flour, mixed with 4 teaspoons baking powder, sifted

ICING

30 g/2½ tablespoons soft dark brown sugar

175 g/1½ sticks butter

300 g/10½ oz. dark/ bittersweet chocolate, chopped

23-cm/9-inch round loose-bottom or springform cake pan, greased and lined with baking parchment

MAKES 1 LARGE CAKE

Julia, one of our bakers at Lola's, spent many years living and working in Australia and still to this day dreams of this dense, intense chocolate cake. She has recreated that memory here in this wonderfully grown-up recipe, that is even more decadent if warmed in the microwave for 30 seconds and served with a large dollop of whipped cream!

Preheat the oven to 160°C (325°F) Gas 3.

Combine the butter, chocolate, 120 ml/½ cup water, cocoa, espresso and vanilla in a medium pan. Cook, whisking constantly, over low heat for 6–8 minutes or until smooth and well combined. Remove from the heat and let stand for 10 minutes or until lukewarm.

Use a hand-held electric whisk to beat the sugar and eggs together in a large mixing bowl until pale and creamy. Whisk in the chocolate mixture until combined. Add the flour and whisk again until combined.

Pour the mixture into prepared cake pan and bake in the preheated oven for 1–1¼ hours or until a skewer inserted into the centre of the cake comes out with crumbs clinging to it. (Do not be concerned if the surface cracks a little).

Allow to cool in the pan for 15 minutes, before turning out onto a wire rack to cool completely.

While the cake is cooling, make the icing. Place 120 ml/½ cup water, brown sugar and butter into a small pan and heat until the mixture begins to melt and bubble. Remove from the heat, add the chopped chocolate and whisk until smooth. Place the pan into cold water to cool a little before scraping out into a bowl. Allow the icing to cool in the fridge for 30–60 minutes until it is a spreadable texture.

Spread the icing all over the cooled cake using a palette knife or metal spatula to make soft swirls in a rustic manner. Leave to stand for 30 minutes or until the icing is firm. When you are ready to serve, cut the cake with a warm knife to prevent the icing from cracking.

Lamingtons AUSTRALIA

A real Australian icon of a cake. Named after Baron Lamington in the late nineteenth century, these scrumptious sponge cakes hide a fruity jam filling and are coated in a dark chocolate and coconut jacket. Perfect with a cup of tea.

250 g/2¼ sticks butter, softened

230 g/1 cup caster/granulated sugar

70 g/⅓ cup plus 1 teaspoon soft light brown sugar

4 eggs

1 teaspoon pure vanilla extract

500 g self-raising flour/3¾ cups cake flour mixed with 8 teaspoons baking powder, sifted

250ml/1 cup full-fat/whole milk

FROSTING

3 tablespoons butter

180 ml/¾ cup whole milk

1 teaspoon pure vanilla extract

80 g/⅔ cup unsweetened cocoa powder

500 g/3½ cups icing/confectioners' sugar

100 g/scant 1½ cups desiccated/dried unsweetened shredded coconut

FILLING

250 ml/1 cup double/heavy cream

1 teaspoon pure vanilla extract

4 tablespoons raspberry jam/jelly or other jam/jelly of your choice

17 x 27-cm/6-½ x 10¾-inch baking pan, greased and lined with baking parchment

MAKES 12 LAMINGTONS

Preheat the oven to 160°C (325°F) Gas 3.

Place the butter and sugar in the bowl of a stand mixer fitted with a whisk attachment (or use a hand-held electric whisk and large mixing bowl) and beat on medium speed until light and fluffy; this should take a couple of minutes. Add the eggs, one at a time, stopping after each addition to scrape down the sides of the bowl. Add the vanilla extract and beat until combined. Add the flour, a little at a time, alternating with the milk, until you have a smooth batter. Do not over-mix.

Spoon into the prepared baking pan and bake in the preheated oven for 30–35 minutes or until springy and well risen. Allow to cool completely in the pan, then remove the sponge from the pan and refrigerate to firm up a little while you make the frosting and filling.

To make the frosting, place the butter, milk and vanilla extract into a small pan and heat to melt the butter into the milk. Sift the cocoa powder and icing/confectioners' sugar into a large mixing bowl (reserve the coconut to use later). Slowly whisk the warm milk into the dry mixture until smooth and glossy. Allow to cool until just warm.

For the filling, whip the cream with the vanilla extract using a hand-held electric whisk (or in a stand mixer) until soft peaks form. Do not over-whip. Place in the fridge until needed.

To assemble the lamingtons, place the coconut onto a large plate. Remove the sponge from the fridge and cut into 12 equal pieces. Carefully use a fork to skewer a sponge piece and dip it into the chocolate frosting, making sure it is fully covered. Allow the excess to drip away and then toss the sponge in the coconut until you have an even covering. Repeat with the remaining pieces. Allow to set for an hour or so at room temperature.

Once set, slice each cake horizontally through the middle to form two even halves. On one half spread a little of your favourite jam/jelly and on the other a generous layer of the filling. Sandwich together and repeat with the other cakes. Then sit back and enjoy the fruits of your labour – yum!

Carrot cake AUSTRALIA

A really light and moist carrot cake that we find ourselves going back to time and time again for a comforting slice. Although found in most countries these days, our favourite carrot cake is based on those tasted on our travels around Australia. Feel free to decorate in your own style – be as adventurous as you dare!

350 ml/scant 1½ cups vegetable oil

350 g/1¾ cups soft light brown sugar

6 eggs

1 teaspoon ground cinnamon

½ whole nutmeg, grated

pinch of ground cloves

250 g/2¼ cups coarsely grated carrots (about 5 medium carrots)

160g/1¼ cups (dark) raisins or sultanas/golden raisins

350 g self-raising flour/ 2⅔ cups cake flour mixed with 5 teaspoons baking powder, sifted

2 teaspoons bicarbonate of soda/baking soda

CREAM CHEESE FROSTING

400 g/14 oz. full-fat cream cheese

100 ml /⅓ cup double/heavy cream

grated zest of 2 oranges

100g/¾ cup icing/ confectioners' sugar, sifted

TO DECORATE

grated or pared zest from 1 orange, pith removed

2 x 23-cm/9-inch round loose-bottom or springform cake pans, greased and lined with baking parchment

MAKES 1 LARGE CAKE

Preheat the oven to 180°C (350°F) Gas 4.

Place the oil, sugar, eggs and spices into a large mixing bowl and whisk until fully combined. Add the grated carrots, raisins, flour and bicarbonate of soda/baking soda and, using a wooden spoon, mix until just combined and there are no traces of flour left.

Divide the batter between the prepared cake pans and spread level, then bake in the preheated oven for 30–40 minutes or until well risen and the cakes spring back to the touch. Remove the cakes from the oven and allow to cool in the pans while you make the frosting.

For the frosting, place the cream cheese and double/heavy cream into the bowl of a stand mixer fitted with the whisk attachment (or use a hand-held electric whisk and large mixing bowl) and whisk until smooth. Add the orange zest and sifted icing/confectioners' sugar and beat again until thickened and fluffy. The mixture will be relatively runny initially, but please persevere as it will thicken and become lovely and light.

Once the cakes are cool, remove from the pans and place one cake onto a serving plate. Spoon one-third of your frosting onto this cake and spread evenly to the edges. Place the other cake on top and gently press down to level. With the remaining frosting, use a palette knife or metal spatula to smooth it all over the top and sides of the cake. You can be as rustic or precise as you choose here. Finally, decorate with grated or pared strips of orange zest. Delicious!

Lolly cake

NEW ZEALAND

This is a really fun cake from New Zealand. We think it's a great recipe to make with your kids, as it requires no baking whatsoever. The recipe is simple but so delicious. Feel free to use nuts and fruits or your favourite chewy candy or lolly to really tailor-make this cake for you and your tastes. We would also say avoid using hard sweets as these will just dissolve into the mixture. Yum!

120 g/1 stick butter

200 g/¾ cup condensed milk

250 g/9 oz. digestive biscuits/ graham crackers, lightly crushed

150 g/5½ oz. gummy sweets/ candies of your choice

100 g/1⅓ cups desiccated/ dried unsweetened shredded coconut

20-cm/8-inch square brownie pan, greased and lined with baking parchment

MAKES 12 PIECES

Start by placing the butter and condensed milk into a pan. Place on low heat and melt together, stirring until fully blended. Remove from the heat and set aside to cool for a few minutes.

Place the crushed biscuits/graham crackers into a bowl with the sweets/candies, add the warm condensed milk mixture and mix using a wooden spoon until fully combined.

Sprinkle half of the coconut into the prepared brownie pan and spread out in an even layer.

Pour the biscuit/graham cracker mixture over the coconut and, using damp hands, push the mix into the pan, making sure to get into all the corners. The coconut will adhere to the crumbs and create a coating. Sprinkle the remaining coconut evenly over the surface and gently press down to coat.

Place the pan into the fridge and allow to set for at least 4 hours or preferably overnight until firm.

Turn the slab out onto a chopping board and cut into 12 pieces.

Pavlova NEW ZEALAND GF

There are so many ways to dress a pavlova. If you ask an Australian it probably has passion fruit and if you ask a New Zealander it might have kiwi fruit. This is our favourite way to dress a 'pav'. Sharp passion fruit and raspberries with sweet strawberries and rich billowing double/heavy cream. Yum!

Preheat the oven to 130°C (250°F) Gas ½.

Place the egg whites, salt and vinegar into the bowl of a stand mixer fitted with the whisk attachment (or use a hand-held electric whisk and large mixing bowl) and whisk on high speed to soft peaks.

Add half of the sugar and whisk on high speed until glossy and stiff peaks form, then add the remaining sugar and the cornflour/cornstarch and whisk until fully combined and you have a meringue that is smooth and glossy.

Spoon the meringue into a circle on the prepared baking sheet, peaking the meringue up slightly around the edges. Bake in the preheated oven for 2 hours until firm and dry (the meringue will not darken at this low heat).

Allow to cool completely on the parchment and then gently slide the meringue onto a serving plate. To assemble, spoon the whipped cream onto the middle of the meringue and gently arrange the raspberries over the cream. Scatter the strawberries over the raspberries and finish with the passion fruit pulp drizzled amongst the fruits. Dust the top of the pavlova with some icing/confectioners' sugar to finish.

3 egg whites

pinch of salt

½ teaspoon white wine vinegar

200 g/1 cup caster/superfine or granulated sugar

1½ teaspoons cornflour/cornstarch, sifted

250 ml/1 cup double/heavy cream, softly whipped

250 g/9 oz. fresh raspberries

250 g/9 oz. fresh strawberries, hulled and quartered

3 passion fruits, pulp only

icing/confectioners' sugar, to decorate

large baking sheet, lined with baking parchment

MAKES 1 LARGE PAVLOVA

Toffee macadamia cake

NEW ZEALAND

CAKE

170 g/1½ sticks butter

275 g/1½ cups minus 2 tablespoons caster/granulated sugar

5 eggs

100 ml/⅓ cup full-fat/whole milk

1½ teaspoons pure vanilla extract

1 teaspoon ground cinnamon

20 g self-raising flour/2⅓ tablespoons cake flour mixed with ⅛ teaspoon baking powder

TOFFEE LAYER

120 ml/½ cup double/heavy cream

190 g/1½ sticks butter

pinch of salt

275 g/1½ cups minus 2 tablespoons soft light brown sugar

50 g/¾ cup desiccated/dried unsweetened shredded coconut, lightly toasted

150 g/1½ cups whole macadamia nuts, lightly toasted

23-cm/9-inch round loose-bottom or springform cake pan, greased and lined with baking parchment

MAKES 1 LARGE CAKE

This cake is truly scrumptious, a real treat. Sticky and dark underneath with the buttery crunch of macadamia nuts and a lightly scented cinnamon sponge on top, this cake is a real crowd-pleaser. Inspired by the wonderful coffee shops of New Zealand, we hope you love this recipe as much as we do.

Preheat the oven to 180°C (350°F) Gas 4.

First, make the toffee layer. Place the cream, butter, salt and brown sugar in a heavy-bottomed pan set over gentle heat. Allow to melt until the sugar has dissolved, then increase the heat and boil for 5 minutes until slightly thickened. Remove from the heat and allow to cool for 10 minutes.

Scatter the toasted coconut and macadamias all over the base of the prepared cake pan. Pour the toffee over the nuts and coconut, then set aside.

To make the cake, place all the cake ingredients into the bowl of a stand mixer fitted with the paddle attachment (or use a hand-held electric whisk and large mixing bowl) and beat on medium speed until well combined and smooth. This is known as an 'all-in-one method' of making a cake batter.

Spoon the batter into the cake pan and spread out with a spatula over the caramelized nut and coconut layer. Bake in the preheated oven for 65–75 minutes or until a skewer inserted into the centre of the cake comes out clean. Allow to cool in the pan for 30 minutes before carefully turning out onto a serving plate. Work carefully as the toffee will still be hot. Peel off the baking parchment and allow to cool before cutting.

Brightly coloured cakes on display at a patisserie in Tokyo (above) and at a bakery in Hong Kong (left).

Novice monks making ceremonial cakes in Bardo Cave Monastery, Yunnan, China (right).

A confectionery counter in
Tokyo, Japan (below).

Geisha walking beneath the cherry
blossoms in Kyoto, Japan (above).

A traditional Chinese mooncake made with
lotus bean paste (above left).

Coconut cake FIJI 🥄🥄

Summery and tropical, this light and airy coconut sponge is finished with a delicious not-too-sweet cream cheese frosting. Conjuring up images of sunsets in the Caribbean and piña coladas.

375 g/2¾ cups plus 1½ tablespoons plain/all-purpose flour

1 teaspoon baking powder

½ teaspoon bicarbonate of soda/baking soda

pinch of salt

450 g/2¼ cups caster/granulated sugar

330 g/3 sticks butter, softened

5 eggs

1½ teaspoons pure vanilla extract

100 g/scant 1½ cups desiccated/dried unsweetened shredded coconut

240 ml/scant 1 cup full-fat/whole milk

CREAM CHEESE FROSTING

60 g/½ stick butter, softened

400 g/14 oz. full-fat cream cheese

½ teaspoon pure vanilla extract

200 g/1½ cups icing/confectioners' sugar, sifted

TO DECORATE

50 g/1 cup shredded or flaked toasted coconut

2 x 23-cm/9-inch round loose-bottom or springform cake pans, greased and lined with baking parchment

MAKES 1 LARGE CAKE

Preheat the oven to 180°C (350°F) Gas 4.

In a large bowl, sift together the flour, baking powder, bicarbonate of soda/baking soda and salt. Set aside.

Place the sugar and butter in the bowl of a stand mixer fitted with a paddle attachment (or use a hand-held electric whisk and large mixing bowl) and beat on medium speed until light and fluffy; this should take a couple of minutes.

Add the eggs, one at a time, stopping after each addition to scrape down the sides of the bowl. Add the vanilla and coconut. Sift in the dry ingredients, a little at a time, alternating with the milk, until the batter is smooth. Do not over-mix.

Divide the batter evenly between the prepared cake pans and bake in the centre of the preheated oven for 35–45 minutes until well risen and a skewer inserted into the centre of the cakes comes out clean.

Remove the cakes from the oven and allow to cool in the pans. When ready to serve, release the cakes from their pans and place the first sponge on a serving plate.

Meanwhile, make the frosting. Place the butter into the bowl of a stand mixer fitted with a whisk attachment (or use a hand-held electric whisk and large mixing bowl) and beat until soft and fluffy. Add the cream cheese and vanilla extract and beat until fully combined. Carefully add the icing/confectioners' sugar (in large spoonfuls to avoid a huge cloud of sugar!) and mix gently to combine. Once fully mixed, beat the icing for a minute or two until light and fluffy.

To assemble the cake, spread half of the frosting evenly over the bottom sponge layer. Place the second sponge on top of this one and top with the remaining frosting. We prefer a rustic look when we frost this cake. Sprinkle over the toasted shredded or flaked coconut to decorate and enjoy.

Matcha cake JAPAN

This is a wonderfully fragrant cake with a light texture. Inspired by our travels in China and Japan, we wanted to create a cake using the wonderful matcha powder that has now become so popular. The white chocolate ganache adds a gentle sweetness to the cake without being overly sweet. If you choose to use green colouring it gives a real eye-catching finish to what we think is an impressive occasion cake.

350 g self-raising flour/2⅔ cups cake flour mixed with 5 teaspoons baking powder

1½ teaspoons baking powder

10 g/2 teaspoons food-grade matcha powder

250 g/2¼ sticks butter, softened

300 g/1½ cups caster/granulated sugar

100g/½ cup soft light brown sugar

1 teaspoon pure vanilla extract

6 eggs

250 g/1 cup sour cream

½ teaspoon green food colouring paste (optional)

WHITE CHOCOLATE GANACHE

80 ml/scant ⅓ cup double/heavy cream

100 g/3½ oz. white chocolate, chopped

1 teaspoon food-grade matcha powder

couple of drops of green food colouring (optional)

26-cm/10½-inch Bundt or decorative ring mould pan, greased and floured

MAKES 1 LARGE CAKE

Preheat the oven to 180°C (350°F) Gas 4.

Sift the flour, baking powder and matcha powder into a large bowl. Set aside until needed.

Place the butter, sugars and vanilla extract into the bowl of a stand mixer fitted with a paddle attachment (or use a hand-held electric whisk and large mixing bowl) and beat on medium speed until fluffy. Add the eggs, one at a time, and mix on low speed until combined, stopping to scrape down the sides of the bowl as you go.

Add the dry sifted ingredients and mix on medium speed until smooth – do not over-mix at this stage. Finally, add the sour cream to the batter and the food colouring, if using.

Pour the batter carefully into the prepared Bundt pan or ring mould and bake in the centre of the preheated oven for 50–55 minutes or until well risen and a skewer inserted into the centre of the cake comes out clean. Allow to cool in the pan for 20 minutes before turning out onto a wire rack to cool completely.

For the ganache, place the double/heavy cream into a pan and heat on medium heat until bubbles start to form around the edge of the pan. Remove from the heat and add the chopped chocolate and matcha powder. Using a whisk, mix until the chocolate has melted and you have a smooth ganache. Add the green colouring, if using. Allow to cool at room temperature until the ganache has thickened but is still a pourable consistency. If this is taking a long time, you can place the ganache into the fridge for 20 minutes or so to help it firm up.

Place the cooled cake onto a serving plate. Using a spoon, carefully pour the ganache over the top of the cake, allowing it to dribble down the sides and find its way into the hole in the centre of the cake. Allow to set for an hour or so before slicing.

Castella cake JAPAN DF 🥄🥄🥄

This Japanese sponge cake has a delightfully bouncy texture due to the gluten in the bread flour. It has a subtle honey flavour that goes so well with a cup of matcha green tea. It is traditional to neatly cut the sides from the loaf once it has been chilled, to reveal the sponge interior for dramatic effect.

Preheat the oven to 160°C (325°F) Gas 3.

In a small bowl, whisk together the honey and warm water and set aside.

Place the eggs into the bowl of a stand mixer fitted with the whisk attachment (or use a hand-held electric whisk and large mixing bowl) and whisk on high speed until combined and frothy. Add the sugar, then beat together on high speed for 5 minutes. You want to create a lot of volume in the eggs. The texture will be thick and the colour will be pale yellow.

Add the honey mixture into the egg mixture and whisk on low speed until combined. Add the strong/bread flour gradually on low speed and beat until just combined, about 1 minute. Do not over-mix.

Pour the batter into the prepared loaf pan and gently tap on the work surface to remove large air bubbles. Bake in the preheated oven for 35–40 minutes or until golden brown and a skewer inserted comes out clean. Remove from the oven.

To finish, mix the honey and warm water in a bowl and brush the mixture over the top of the hot cake with a pastry brush. Allow to soak in for a minute or two.

Place a large sheet of clingfilm/plastic wrap onto the work surface. Turn the cake out of the pan and place directly onto the clingfilm/plastic wrap, top down. Peel off the parchment paper. Immediately wrap the hot cake with clingfilm/plastic wrap and place in the fridge overnight. This will help the cake to stay moist and keep its shape.

Remove the cake from the fridge and unwrap when ready to serve. Cut into thick slices with a sharp bread knife and enjoy. You can also cut off the sides to expose the white interior if you want to serve this cake the traditional Japanese way.

75 g/¼ cup runny honey
2½ tablespoons warm water
6 eggs
220 g/1 cup plus 1 tablespoon caster/granulated sugar
½ teaspoon pure vanilla extract
200 g/1½ cups white strong/bread flour, sifted twice

TO FINISH

1 tablespoon runny honey
½ tablespoon warm water

24 x 15-cm/9½ x 6-inch loaf pan, greased and lined with baking parchment

MAKES 1 LOAF CAKE

Sesame cake

INDIA

This nutty and delicious cake really showcases the flavour of sesame. It has a slightly chewy texture and is not overly sweet, therefore it lends itself to being served with a delicious vanilla ice cream and drizzled with honey. We think you will enjoy this Eastern delight.

120 g/1 cup minus 1 tablespoon plain/all-purpose flour, sifted

½ teaspoon bicarbonate of soda/baking soda

½ teaspoon baking powder

pinch of salt

80 g/¾ stick butter, softened

135 g/scant ¾ cup caster/granulated sugar

2 eggs

1 teaspoon pure vanilla extract

30 g/⅛ cup runny honey

140 ml/¾ cup full-fat/whole milk

50 g/⅓ cup sesame seeds (you can also use black sesame seeds if you prefer)

15 g/⅛ cup poppy seeds

23-cm/9-inch round loose-bottom or springform cake pan, greased and lined with baking parchment

MAKES 1 LARGE CAKE

Preheat the oven to 180°C (350°F) Gas 4.

Start by combining the flour, bicarbonate of soda/baking soda, baking powder and salt in a mixing bowl.

Place the butter and sugar into the bowl of a stand mixer fitted with the paddle attachment (or use a hand-held electric whisk and large mixing bowl) and beat on medium speed until light and fluffy. Beat in the eggs one at a time, on medium speed, stopping to scrape down the sides of the bowl as you go. Stir in the vanilla extract and honey.

Add the flour mixture and mix well until combined. Do not over-mix. Slowly pour in the milk and mix until the batter is smooth. Finally, stir in the sesame and poppy seeds.

Pour the batter into the prepared cake pan and bake in the preheated oven for 35–40 minutes until golden and a skewer inserted into the centre of the cake comes out clean. Allow to cool in the pan completely before serving.

We like to drizzle each slice of cake with a little honey and serve with a large scoop of ice cream – a truly delicious treat!

Mango cake BURMA

Inspired by the tropical climate of Burma and the abundance of fresh fruit (in particular the fragrant mango), we have created this rather special teatime treat. Scented with mango pulp, the sponge is a gorgeous orange hue. We have then sandwiched the cakes with double/heavy cream and more fragrant mango flesh, along with a hint of lime zest to lift the cake. We find it is best to use very ripe mangoes that have been strained once puréed, or if out of season, canned mango pulp will work just as well.

Preheat the oven to 160°C (325°F) Gas 3.

First, you need to strain the puréed mango pulp to give a very smooth consistency. Discard the fibrous mango pulp left in the sieve/strainer. Set aside 3 tablespoons of the strained purée for the filling/topping and put the remaining smooth purée into the bowl of a stand mixer fitted with the paddle attachment (or use a hand-held electric whisk and large mixing bowl).

Add all the other cake ingredients to the bowl. This is what is known as an all-in-one method of making a cake batter. Beat together until well combined and smooth. Do not over-mix. Spoon the mixture into the prepared cake pan and spread out with a spatula. Bake in the preheated oven for 45–50 minutes or until a skewer inserted into the centre comes out clean. Allow the cake to cool in the pan for 20 minutes before turning out onto a wire rack to cool completely.

To make the filling/topping, place the double/heavy cream, icing/confectioners' sugar and lime juice into the bowl of a stand mixer fitted with the whisk attachment (or use a hand-held electric whisk and large mixing bowl) and whip until soft peaks form. This may take a few minutes but be careful not to over-whip as the cream will split and separate. Once softly whipped, fold through most of the reserved mango purée, reserving a little of the purée for decoration.

Using a serrated knife, slice horizontally through the middle of the cake to create two even layers. Take two-thirds of the cream mixture and spread over one of the sponges. Place the next sponge layer on top and gently press down. Use a spatula to smooth the remaining cream mixture over the top of the cake and create some rough swirls. Decorate the cake with slices of fresh ripe mango and a drizzle of any remaining mango purée. Serve immediately.

400 g/1½ cups puréed mango pulp

335 g/1¾ cups caster/granulated sugar

2 eggs

335 g/2½ cups plain/all-purpose flour

1¼ teaspoons baking powder

½ teaspoon pure vanilla extract

FILLING/TOPPING

350 ml/scant 1½ cups double/heavy cream

50 g/generous ⅓ cup icing/confectioners' sugar, sifted

1 tablespoon freshly squeezed lime juice

DECORATION

½ fresh mango, sliced

23-cm/9-inch round loose-bottom or springform cake pan, greased and lined with baking parchment

MAKES 1 LARGE CAKE

Honey cake RUSSIA 🥄🥄🥄

The Russian honey cake is a classic pâtisserie staple and can often be up to fifteen layers tall. This version contains just eight layers, but still has massive impact. Turn to pages 186–187 to read more about this stunning cake.

CAKE
60 g/¼ cup runny honey
150 g/¾ cup caster/granulated sugar
30 g/¼ stick butter
3 eggs, beaten
1 teaspoon baking powder

400 g/3 cups plain/all-purpose flour, sifted, plus extra for dusting

FILLING/TOPPING
240 ml/1 cup double/heavy cream
700 ml/2⅔ cups sour cream
1 tablespoon runny honey

120 g/1 cup icing/confectioners' sugar, sifted

2 large baking sheets, lined with baking parchment
23-cm/9-inch round cake board or base to use as a template

MAKES 1 LARGE CAKE

Preheat the oven to 180°C (350°F) Gas 4.

For the cake, place the honey, sugar and butter into a heatproof bowl set over a pan of simmering water. Melt over low-medium heat, whisking occasionally for about 5 minutes or until the sugar has melted. Immediately remove from the heat and allow to cool for 5 minutes before vigorously whisking in the the beaten eggs until incorporated.

Whisk in the baking powder and then gradually fold in the flour with a spatula until the dough comes together and becomes too hard to mix with a spatula. You may not need all of the flour or you may need a little extra if the dough is too sticky. Cut the dough into eight equal pieces.

On a well-floured surface, roll one piece of dough out into a thin 23-cm/9-inch rough circle. This can be tricky as the dough will be very thin. Sprinkle the top with a little flour if it's sticking to the rolling pin. Use the rolling pin to transfer the rough circle to one of the prepared baking sheets. Repeat the process with another ball of dough and bake in the preheated oven, two at a time, for 4–5 minutes until golden. Transfer to a wire rack and let cool completely before stacking. Repeat with the remaining dough. Leave the oven on.

Using the 23-cm/9-inch cake board as a template, cut each of the eight baked layers into a neat circle. Keep the off-cuts and place them back in the oven for another 5 minutes to brown a little. Remove from the oven and let cool completely before processing to fine crumbs in a blender. These will be used as decoration.

For the filling/topping, whip the cream to stiff peaks with a hand-held electric whisk or in a stand mixer. In a separate bowl, whisk together the sour cream, honey and icing/confectioners' sugar. Fold in the whipped cream and set aside.

To assemble, spread a little filling onto a serving plate and use to secure the first cake layer. Spread a good amount of the filling over the first layer. Add another layer, gently pressing down to get rid of any air. Continue layering the cake and generously filling until you have a stack of eight layers. Smooth the remaining filling over the top and sides with a palette knife or metal spatula.

Sprinkle the crumbs over the top and sides of the cake, cover loosely with clingfilm/plastic wrap and refrigerate overnight. (Don't be tempted to skip this stage as the filling needs to soak in.) Remove from the fridge an hour before serving.

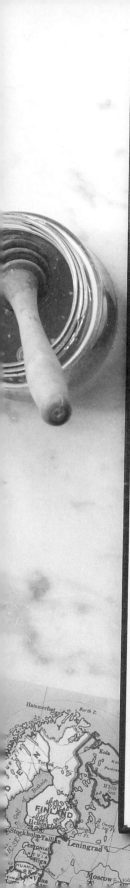

Honey cake: a royal Russian treat

Known within Russia as Medovik Tort, the Honey Cake is so adored by Russian citizens that it is a popular choice for pride of place at celebrations and special occasions. Outside of Russia, the recipe is not as well-known, though those who taste it tend to be instantly charmed by its neat layers and delicate, delicious flavour.

The cake comprises of a stack of soft, sweet cookie layers – there can be as little as four or as many as 15 piled high. Our version has a manageable but still impressive eight layers, though you can adjust this to suit, making a little more or less filling as needed. The layers are sandwiched together with a luscious creamy caramel frosting. There are seemingly hundreds of different variations of this frosting: some are made with sour cream, others with whipped cream. Some are sweetened with boiled condensed milk, others with honey or icing/confectioners sugar. We think we have cracked the perfect combination with a mixture of double/ heavy cream, sour cream, icing/ confectioners' sugar and a little honey. The most crucial step of the recipe is that

the cake is left to soak in the frosting overnight in the fridge, giving a moist, but not soggy or disintegrating texture. Toppings for the cake can include crushed walnuts or fresh berries, to provide a contrast in texture. We have suggested the traditional topping of crunchy baked cookie off-cuts, but you can add to this as you wish. The overall flavour of the cake can be described as somewhere between stroopwafel, dobos torte, caramel graham cracker or speculoos cookie spread.

There are many cakes in this book that feature honey; it is the oldest sweetener in existence, but it brings its own unique flavour that modern sweeteners cannot compete with. The Ancient Egyptians used it to sweeten many dishes, and it has been a prominent ingredient in Russian cooking since pagan times, for example, used in gingerbread, the making of mead, and also medicinally. The origin of the first Medovik Tort is not known for sure, but the tale goes that a young confectioner created the recipe for Empress Elizabeth, wife of Emperor Alexander I, in Russia in the 1820s. The Empress had a particular dislike for honey, and this was widely known throughout the royal court. The bold young chef (bravely or foolishly) came up with a recipe for a delicious cake with a honey-based dough. The flavour of the cake was so sublime that Empress Elizabeth loved the cake and demanded the chef be brought in front of her to ask exactly how it was made. The poor chef, ready to accept his fate, had to confess that the cake was made with honey. But instead of being punished, he was rewarded. From then on, Medovik graced the tables of nobility and later on the rest of the population. It became popular with the people because of the simplicity of the ingredients that combine to create this truly stunning cake.

Index

Picture credits

Acknowledgements

With thanks to all the hard-working bakers, decorators and the rest of the Lola's team in the bakery and stores who all contribute to making Lola's a fun and exciting place to work. Special thanks to Julia Head, a crucial part of the Lola's creative team, who developed and tested the recipes in this book. Having worked on Lola's Forever (2014) and having travelled extensively herself, Julia was the perfect choice to help us create this book of delicious international recipes. Thanks to Cathy Seward for Americanizing and testing the recipes. Thank you to Steve Painter and Lucy McKelvie for bringing the recipes to life with stunning photography. Finally, thank you to Cindy Richards, Julia Charles, Leslie Harrington, Patricia Harrington, Alice Sambrook and all at Ryland Peters & Small for producing such a beautiful book.